# Hey Waiter, There's An Umbrella In My Drink!

# Hey Waiter,
## There's An Umbrella In My Drink!

TALES FROM THE TROPICS
BY HAWAI'I'S FAVORITE HUMORIST

## CHARLES MEMMINGER

WATERMARK
PUBLISHING

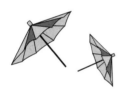

© 2006 Charles Memminger

ISBN 0-9779143-1-3

Library of Congress Control Number:
2006928562

Watermark Publishing
1088 Bishop Street, Suite 310
Honolulu, HI 96813
Telephone: Toll-free 1-866-900-BOOK
Web site: www.bookshawaii.net
e-mail: sales@bookshawaii.net

Printed in the United States

# Contents

*For my wife Margie, daughter Sarah, dog Boomer, lovebird Sweetie, the other lovebird whose name escapes me, and all the various ants, roaches, geckos and mongooses who have played important roles in my writing, not to mention my life in general*

# Foreword

I don't know what you were expecting when you picked up *Hey Waiter, There's An Umbrella In My Drink!*—but you're in for a real treat. I've known Charley for a long time and truly enjoy his writing. The great thing about his observations is that they're like leftovers: better the second time around. He is insightful, bright, honest, intelligent and damn funny, which to me matters more than those first four qualities.

Charley has managed to write not only a very entertaining book (you'll find yourself laughing out loud, which is quite all right) but one that gives us an up-close-and-personal look at life and local customs in the Hawaiian Islands. It's a must-read for anyone who wants to get an honest glimpse of the real Hawai'i.

Charley's Hawai'i perspective comes naturally. He attended high school in the Islands but has lived all over the world, gaining the kind of seasoning that's helped make him an award-winning humor columnist and screenwriter. While much of his material is about life in the Aloha State, it's written in a context that stretches far beyond Hawai'i's shores. (I told you he was intelligent.)

Charley asked me not to use the phrase "the Dave Barry of Hawai'i"—which I had never thought of using until he told me not to. (Do not mention a pink elephant.) Well, he's not—he's so much more! He is "the Charles Memminger of Hawai'i," and it doesn't get any better than that. We love Charley and his humor—and the way it helps us keep our sanity. You'll feel the same way after you've read this delightful collection of his columns.

My favorite story in the book is the title piece—*Hey Waiter, There's An Umbrella In My Drink!* What's yours?

Aloha,
Wally Amos
Cookieman and author
(*Be Positive! Be Positive!, The Power in You*)
www.chipandcookie.com

# About the Author

Charles Memminger is a national award-winning columnist for the *Honolulu Star-Bulletin*. His column, "Honolulu Lite," has twice been named the top humor column in the country (for newspapers under 100,000 circulation, that is) by the National Society of Newspaper Columnists (three of the nicest guys you'll ever meet).

His work also has been distributed (albeit without payment) by the New York Times News Service, and he has been published in *Newsweek, Better Homes & Gardens, OMNI*, the *Boston Globe* and other national publications. He has also won several screenwriting competitions (though admittedly has never actually sold a screenplay) and was a staff writer for "Baywatch Hawaii," one of the longest running shows on television. (The show's cancellation shortly after he was hired is purely coincidental.) He is author of the book (well, more like a booklet) *Hey Tourist! Buy This Book!* His essays were included in *Chicken Soup for the Soul of America* and *Chicken Soup from the Soul of Hawaii* (though he admits to never having actually read a *Chicken Soup* book.)

Memminger lives in Kaneohe, Hawai'i, with his wife, Margie, daughter, Sarah, and various birds, dogs and other creatures, great and small, who play recurring roles in his writing.

SARAH MEMMINGER

# Introduction

As an Air Force brat, I saw the world. And the world was weird. Born in Florida, I found myself in Morocco at age five. Then we moved to Georgia, where I was the only kid who could speak Arabic. Then we moved to Nebraska, where I was considered a southern "Rebel." Then we moved to Alabama, where I was a Yankee. When my Dad returned from Vietnam we moved to Hawai'i. Finally, I thought, I would be normal. I would live in a true melting pot. It wasn't long after getting off the airplane that I first heard the phrase, "Hey, haole!"

So, yes, I was now an Arab Rebel Yankee Haole. But I learned that haole wasn't a derogatory term unless preceded by the type of modifier we can't go into here. Haole simply meant Caucasian. And to be haole in Hawai'i was to be part of the great mixed plate of diverse cultures and ethnicities: Hawaiian, Filipino, haole, Japanese, Chinese, Samoan, Tongan, black, (insert your ethnicity here), and usually several different flavors at once. And for a writer, Hawai'i was an enormous calabash bowl of unique cultures, eccentricities, wildlife, ocean life, plant life and, well, life life. After decamping to Oregon to go to college and then to West Virginia and Guam (yes, I've been to all the garden spots) to work at newspapers, I returned to Hawai'i in 1980 to work at the *Honolulu Star-Bulletin*. After stints as a reporter covering crime, courts, investigative reporting and feature writing, I launched a column called "Honolulu Lite" in 1991. This was to be a little experiment in journalism, an attempt to bring a smile to the faces of the smileless, to tug at the heartstrings and other bodily viscera of those with hearts and viscera, to boldly go where no column had ever gone before, with as little litigation as possible.

And I think we've done that. At least the lawyers seem happy. With this book I offer some of my favorite columns about Hawai'i, life and everything else. I feel lucky to have been accepted into this crazy, weird, lovable, mixed up, special place called the Hawaiian Islands. And I've finally come to grips with my inner outsider. I am home. Now, when some sees me and calls out "Hey, haole!" I take it as a term of endearment, and rarely flinch.

Aloha,
Charles Memminger

one
---
# Only in Hawai'i

*"Hawai'i is a unique state. It is a small state.*
*It is a state that is by itself. It is different from the other 49 states.*
*Well, all states are different, but it's got a particularly unique situation."*
—U.S. Vice President Dan Quayle

I think Dan put his finger on it. What can you say about the most beautiful state in the country? And yet various polls tend to say we have the worst weather because it tends to rain a little bit here. As I keep pointing out, the difference between Oregon and Hawai'i is that our rain is *warm*. Honolulu also has a famous mountain that everyone thinks is named after a thirsty Greek god but is actually named after a mere mortal who cooked up his own son and served it to Zeus and his buddies. Some other "only in Hawai'i"s? We're the only state that encourages reptiles (geckos) to live in our homes to feed on other intruders. We're the only island state, and yet we have "interstate highways." We're the only state to have both snow (at the 13,000-foot level of Mauna Kea) and hurricanes at the same time. And let's not even talk about what people eat here. As Dan Quayle might say, "all states are different, but Hawai'i is the differentest."

# The Art of Extreme Eating

*(With translations for our Island visitors)*

W
hen is the government going to learn that Hawai'i residents are thrill-seekers when it comes to food? We like our eggs runny, our hot food cold, our cold food warm, our musubi three days old at room temperature and our takeout Zippy's chili to sit in the back of the refrigerator until it's got a little head of green, fuzzy hair. (Musubi is rice-and-anything wrapped with seaweed, as long as the "anything" is Spam, hot dog, tuna or kimchi.)

Macaroni salad isn't ready for consumption until it's sat in the hot sun on a picnic table for a couple of hours. Damn the mayo, full feed ahead! Double- and triple-dipping huli-huli chicken in the same sauce? Chance 'em, brah. Go for it! (Macaroni salad is merely mayo and elbow noodles. Even I don't understand why anyone eats it. Huli-huli chicken is cooked huli-huli style, or turned over a lot with tongs on the fire.)

Salmonella is just another condiment, like that open bottle of shoyu that hasn't seen the inside of a refrigerator in three years. That shoyu isn't old; it's aged, like fine wine. (Salmonella has nothing to do with salmon, unless the salmon's been sitting on a park bench in the sun for a week. Shoyu is soy sauce. Soy sauce and shoyu allegedly have nothing in common with Soylent Green.)

Let's not even talk about rice. A rice pot can sit on a counter for days, and the rice will set up its own force field against bacteria. At least it will if it's local rice, rice that can hold together in a solid lump to fight off the enemy spirochetes and invading spores. With Uncle Ben's rice, each grain is separate, independent and vulnerable to viral attack. (Uncle Ben's rice is a white food-like product eaten on the mainland with gravy.)

We like our fish raw, our hamburger blood-rare and our pork cooked in the dirt with hot rocks. Sure, undercooked hamburger and runny eggs are dangerous. We don't need the federal government to tell us that. We thrive on extreme cuisine in the Islands. We'll take that week-old rice, top it with that undercooked hamburger and runny egg and smother the whole mess with gravy and call it loco moco. It's not dangerous, it's *breakfast*. Because we are living la vida loco moco, my friend. (A loco moco is the breakfast concoction described above. It was invented by a very confused chef on the Big Island after his microwave blew up. Actually, during his microwave blowing up. To be truthful, *causing* his microwave to blow up.)

You catch a fish off the reef that might have some toxin that will never leave your body for the rest of your life? Toss that buggah on the hibachi. What's a little nerve or liver damage when it comes to ono pupus? (A hibachi is a tiny, annoying charcoal cooker unleashed on the world by a sadistic Japanese barbeque chef. Pupus are any tiny food cooked on a hibachi that doesn't fall through the grill.)

The federal weenies can take their warnings about eating runny eggs and hang 'em up with ducks in Chinatown. A state law requiring Spam musubi to be refrigerated? Are you mad? Spam has an unrefrigerated half-life longer than plutonium. Spam is *embalmed* with salt. If they had buried an open can of Spam with King Tut, it would still be edible today, not to mention tasty. (Spam musubi actually has a half-life longer than uranium 235.)

In Japan they are selling something called "Godzilla Meat." It's actually canned corned beef, which is more dangerous than actual giant angry-dinosaur meat any day. In Hawai'i we eat canned corned beef from Ecuador, man. God knows what's actually in that stuff, because they don't even raise cows in that country. It must be King Kong Meat or something. (Giant-angry-dinosaur meat reportedly does not taste like chicken.)

But it's all good. Eating dried plum pits that have sat in giant jars at Ala Moana Shopping Center for decades is a test of will that no other state in the country would attempt. Raw squid that has been dried and shredded up into nasty, gnarly-looking yellow strings is chewed like gum. Wait for fruit to ripen? No way, pal. Pick those mangoes green and soak 'em a year in vinegar. Pickled mango! 'Ono Sonny Bono, brah. (Dried salty pits of plums and other fruits are called "crack seed" in Hawai'i. But you cannot plant them and grow crack. 'Ono means "yummy" except when used in the same sentence as 'Yoko.')

Still looking for action? Risk being beaten to death by waves to pry thorny little 'opihi from lava rocks so you can suck 'em up with beer. ('Opihi are small shellfish, like clams the size of thumbnails, that cling stubbornly onto rocks on the shore. Dangerous waves often break on these rocks, injuring 'opihi pickers but amusing the 'opihi immensely.)

Spare us your health warnings. Pass the pickled pigs' feet, the balut and the fish roe the size of marbles. We celebrate the most dangerous food in the world. This is Hawai'i. (You don't want to know what balut is. Trust me.)

# Hawai'i: Ready for Its Close-up

It's not every day you get to dress up as an enormous penguin—especially in Hawai'i, where tuxedos are more costumes than actual clothes. But I was asked to emcee the Hawaii Theatre's annual fund-raiser, which was billed as a celebration of the history of Hollywood in Hawai'i. Attendees were supposed to get dolled up as though they were going to a Hollywood premiere, but it's hard to get your hands on the really freaky clothes that are essential to that kind of a shindig.

So I settled for a long-tailed tux with a sort of Horatio Hornblower 19th-century naval vest thing going on in front. "Dashing" is a word often used to describe people who dress up in this kind of serious rental apparel, but in my case the operational word remained "penguin."

But hosting the event gave me a chance to dig into the history of filming in Hawai'i, and I managed to uncover some pretty interesting bits of trivia. Like, after shooting *Blue Hawaii* here, Elvis Presley actually said, "Poi is the only thing I don't like about Hawai'i." That took a lot of guts coming from a guy who considered deep-fried peanut butter sandwiches high cuisine.

The first notable movie shot in Hawai'i was *Hula*, in 1927, starring sexy Clara Bow as the daughter of a Big Island rancher. Infamous beach boy Duke Kahanamoku played a small part in the film but apparently a much larger part with the females in the cast. If you catch my drift.

In the 1930s, *Waikiki Wedding* was a smash hit, with Bing Crosby. A very young Anthony Quinn played a character named Kimo. Apparently, the role of Zorba the Hawaiian was taken.

The film *Bird of Paradise*, starring sex kitten Delores Del Rio, was shot in 1932. Producer David O. Selznick actually told the director, "I don't care what story you use, so long as we call it *Bird of Paradise* and Del Rio jumps into a flaming volcano at the finish." That pretty much set the tone for many Hawai'i movies to come.

In 1939 Eleanor Powell, in the film *Honolulu*, became the first person to do the hula in tap shoes. What possessed her to do it, I don't know. And I'm happy to report that I've never actually seen it.

Then in 1942, Hilo Hattie made her screen debut in the movie *Song of the Islands*, singing "The Cockeyed Mayor of Kaunakakai." You don't see too many songs making fun of visually handicapped public servants anymore.

Elvis made a number of movies here, including *Girls, Girls, Girls*! I believe it was a sequel to the lightly regarded *Girls, Girls*. Then again, maybe not.

*From Here to Eternity*, in 1953, had a star-studded cast. Producer Buddy Adler allegedly told the director, "I don't care what story you use as long as Ernest Borgnine jumps off a flaming Montgomery Clift at the finish." Then again, maybe he didn't.

But there were truly a number of stinkers made in Hawai'i. In 1958 someone shot *She Gods of Shark Reef*, starring...well, who the hell cares? Twenty years later, someone else made *Aloha Donnie and Marie*. The less said about that the better. Even Hawai'i can't save a Donnie and Marie movie.

# Thar She Blows

From May to November it's officially hurricane season in the tropics, a time when we get to see which parts of the Pacific Rim God likes and which ones he hates.

I don't believe God actually hates certain areas, but a lot of people do. When Hurricane 'Iniki smashed into Kaua'i in 1992, many O'ahu residents said, "God spared us," as if God somehow had it in for the good people of Kaua'i.

Anyway, there are certain things you can do to prepare for hurricane season in Hawai'i, the most practical of which is to move to Las Vegas. If you insist on staying, here are some tips from Charley's Not-Quite-Complete Hurricane Survival Guide:

- Check to see if you have a supply of fresh batteries. The key word here is fresh. The batteries you've had in your portable CD player, hand-held poker machine and remote-control racecar for the past year are not fresh. Put brand-new batteries in those and other small appliances because, once your house is blown away, you're going to need some entertainment.
- Check to see if you have any loose boards, plywood, broken lawn furniture or other dangerous materials sitting in your yard. These can become missiles in high winds. Quietly drop these items over the fence into your neighbor's yard.
- Secure large picture windows with masking tape. This won't keep them from breaking but will amuse your neighbors.
- Have a well-maintained, gas-powered generator handy to keep essential appliances running, such as the refrigerator in the garage that holds the beer.
- Have a well-maintained high-powered rifle handy to keep jealous neighbors at bay when they spy you having a cold, frosty brew during the storm.
- Attach cats, dogs and other outdoor pets to lānai railings with surfboard leashes. (Goggles optional).
- Obtain a week's supply of pet tranquilizers from the vet.

You'll need them. Your animals won't. But you will.

- Fill your kitchen cabinets and cupboards with cans of Spam. First of all, it is a federal law that you have Spam on hand during a natural disaster, and secondly, the sheer weight of the Spam stash might keep the house pinned down during high winds.
- Have plenty of extra cash on hand because, after the storm, bribery will be the most efficient way to do business.

**After the storm:**
- Count heads to make sure everyone is safe. Once the heads are counted, make sure there are corresponding bodies to go with them. If you find any extra heads and/or bodies, check with your neighbors to see if they are missing anyone and/or any body parts.
- Check the condition of your house. If an empty lot occupies the spot where your house used to be, then the condition of your house is "Gone."
- If your house is there but you aren't sure whether it's structurally sound, find a wolf passing by and ask him to huff and puff and try to blow it down. If he can't, it's probably safe to go in. But let your neighbor go in first.
- If everyone is safe and the house is OK, stow the firearms, crank up the CD player and hand out the beer because it's Party Time! Unless it's still May. In that case, make a plane reservation for Las Vegas.

# Menehune Not a Myth?

It's appropriate on this Halloween Day that we consider the recent discovery of a tiny species of human that lived on an Indonesian island along with rats the size of dogs, lizards the size of alligators and elephants the size of ponies.

Some suspect that Flores Island was a repository for God's early attempts at making animals. (God: There. I've made rat. Hey, that doesn't look right. If I make the rat that big, how big am I going to have to make a cat? And the elephant, I'm not pleased with him, either. Note to Gene Fabrication Department: Make elephant bigger. As big as the hamster we made last week. And when you're done with that, make the hamster smaller. The size of a pony. Durn, this is harder than I thought it was going to be.)

But it's true—the part about the tiny humans and weird animals, not the part about God. Scientists just discovered the remains of three-foot-high humans, which they've nicknamed "Hobbits," because, you know, when you make a discovery that completely changes human history, it's always good to belittle the discovery by naming it after a silly made-up creature from a book.

The little people lived around 18,000 years ago, and no one knows why they died out. It could be that they simply evolved downward over thousands of years until they disappeared. On the other hand, when you're that tiny and you live on a little island with rats the size of dogs and lizards the size of alligators, culinary accidents do happen. But the cool thing about this discovery is it makes it possible that stories of little people around the world aren't just myths, but true history. There really could have been leprechauns dancing around Ireland with bowls of magically delicious Lucky Charms cereal. And Hawai'i really might have been populated by menehune, the legendary shy yet industrious forest-dwellers.

Legend has it that Kaua'i was simply teeming with menehune who built walls and fishponds, many of which still stand today. It is possible that menehune are descendants of the Flores little people who sailed to Hawai'i in double-hulled canoes the size of golf carts.

You can just imagine when they first landed on, say, Moloka'i and remarked, "Wow, what a BIG island." Then they landed on O'ahu and said, "Now THIS is a big island." And when they finally landed on the Big Island, they were just speechless. It's a small world, sure—unless you are only three feet tall.

The menehune apparently didn't bring any of the exotic Flores animals with them. So we were lucky there. When you've got cockroaches the size of a slipper, you don't need any dog-size rats.

They probably lived happy lives, building walls and digging ditches because, you know, you can never have too many of those. According to legend, they liked dancing, singing and archery. In that order. Which explains why many menehune celebrations ended in bloodshed.

The menehune were probably stomped out, literally, when the Polynesians arrived. (Hey, who are those big guys?) The Flores Island discovery should now lead to a hunt for menehune remains on Kaua'i. How hard can it be? If you find a bow or arrow the size of a chopstick, you're on the right track.

# Encyclopedia Hawaiiana

U pon completion of the *Encyclopedia Memmingerica* (a work in progress), you will find the following salient facts about A.J. Jacobs:

- He's editor-at-large for *Esquire Magazine*.
- He read the entire *Encyclopedia Britannica* and wrote a book about the experience called *The Know-It-All (One Man's Humble Quest to Become the Smartest Person in the World)*.
- Despite reading the entire encyclopedia, the best he could do on the TV game show *Who Wants to Be a Millionaire?* was to win $1,000.
- The answer to the $32,000 question that tripped him up was "red blood cells." (What component of blood is also known as an erythrocyte?)
- While millions of important facts are to be gleaned from the *Encyclopedia Britannica*, A.J. tended to have the more bizarre ones stick in his brain: for example, elephant copulation lasts 20 seconds, French philosopher Rene Descartes adored cross-eyed women and Edgar Allen Poe married his 13-year-old first cousin.
- A.J. is the kind of guy I've got to meet.

My daughter gave me a copy of A.J.'s book for Christmas, and I devoured it. It is part-memoir and part horn o' plenty, this horn being filled with amazing facts—like, the urine of humans and Dalmatian dogs is strangely similar. And opossums have 13 nipples.

The sole Hawaiʻi reference in his book was this: "Ukulele: The Hawaiian ukulele is adapted from the Portuguese machada and is quite unsuited to indigenous musical forms. In other words, Don Ho's 'Tiny Bubbles' is not an ancient Pacific island chant. Disillusioning."

That's pretty funny. And I wish I'd thought of it. So not only did I want to meet this guy A.J., I wanted to find out what other facts and insights he found in the encyclopedia about Hawaiʻi.

I figured the chance of me actually getting in contact with an editor of *Esquire* was slim, but I gave it a shot. I sent an e-mail to an address I found on the Internet. Just so A.J. wouldn't think I was some kook or weirdo, I introduced myself as "the biggest newspaper humor columnist in the Pacific, weighing in at about 250 pounds."

Since I knew he was fond of the fact that many famous people in history have married their cousins, I pointed out a fact from the evolving *Encyclopedia Memmingerica* that not only were the parents of French impressionist Henri Toulouse-Lautrec first cousins, but their parents were first cousins. And that might be why the Toulouse-Lautrec family in old photos looks like a circus act.

Amazingly, A.J. wrote back the next day. "I loved your note! That Toulouse-Lautrec fact is excellent." So I'm glad I went with that fact instead of, say, something about Hawaiian geckos being parthenogenic (the females don't need to have sex to lay fertilized eggs).

A.J. searched his notes from his reading of the *Encyclopedia Britannica* and sent me the following Hawai'i tidbits:

- "I'iwi: The word with the highest percentage of I's in the entire encyclopedia—an impressive 75%. It's a Hawaiian songbird."
- "Hawaiian missionaries banned surfing in the 19th century because it encouraged the intermingling of the sexes. You saw *Blue Crush*—you know what I'm talking about."
- "Francisco de Paula Marin: A horticultural experimenter who introduced many plant species to the Hawaiian islands, including peaches and oranges. He was also known for refusing to share his bountiful crops with friends. So the Hawaiian corruption of his name—Manini—is slang for 'miserly.'"
- "Mauna Loa, Earth's largest volcano, is pretty big. But it ain't no Olympus Mons, which is Mars' biggest volcano, which is twice as high (88,000 feet)."

Excellent! Now if the encyclopedia would just include the Hawaiian word i'i, which I think is a type of seal, Hawai'i would claim a word with 100% I's.

It's also kind of fitting that "Manini," the name of the tightwad Spanish horticulturist who introduced so many alien species to Hawai'i, also became the name of a little fish much consumed by Hawaiian royalty.

So, thanks for the info, A.J. If *Who Wants to Be a Millionaire?* ever includes Hawai'i trivia, we'll all be ready. In the meantime, the *Encyclopedia Memmingerica*—like its author—continues to expand. Did you know that Korean dictator Syngman Rhee, Charles Lindberg, Nobel Prize winner Georg von Bekesy and Ferdinand Marcos all died in Hawai'i? That might not be as interesting as how long it takes an elephant to copulate, but it's good to know.

# Accidents Will Happen, Dude

B ritain's Department of Health recently released a report on "unusual accidents" that landed United Kingdom residents in the hospital in 2004. They included:

- 22 people injured from melting of nightwear, most of them men.
- 1,839 who fell out of trees.
- Four people bitten by venomous centipedes or spiders.
- A girl bitten by an alligator in her pajamas. (How he got in her pajamas, nobody knows.)
- A prince bitten by a venomous, dowdy duchess. (Wait, that was last week.)

This got me wondering about unusual accidents in Hawai'i last year. Here's what I uncovered:

- 27 people injured in "poi-related accidents."
- Nine people hit by falling coconuts, all while shopping at one particular supermarket.
- One supermarket fruit and produce stock boy kicked in the behind by a manager and told to "knock it off with the coconuts."
- Three Waikīkī prostitutes injured by bounced checks.
- A surfer beaten up by a band of bruddahs for "excessive and gratuitous use of the word 'dude.'"
- A boy bitten by a mongoose in his pajamas. (Authorities know how the mongoose got into his pajamas but aren't saying.)
- 4,534 drivers who suffered simultaneous and continuous whiplash while following an SUV driver listening to conga music.
- 14 spiders and centipedes bitten by venomous children.
- One depressed yet confused man slightly injured after trying to kill himself by jumping off the Pali Golf Course. (Note to visitors: the golf course is flat. Get it? You can't jump off of it. Never mind.)

- 23 people injured by marine life, mostly at the Kaneohe Marine Base. (How weird is that?)
- 38 voters hurt by falling hyperbole while touring the State Legislature.
- 29 participants in a Big Island New Age retreat who suffered serious burns during "Increase Your Self-Esteem and Confidence Barefoot Hot Lava Walk."
- A Waikīkī beachgoer who suffered dangerous toxic lack of sunshine after wearing sunscreen with SPF Level 4,000.
- A mongoose bitten by a boy in his pajamas. (How the boy got in the mongoose's pajamas, nobody knows.)

# Hawai'i Burned on Weather Survey

Yuma, Arizona, has better weather than Honolulu? Yuma? Where automobiles come equipped with spatulas so you can detach your sizzling fried backside from the driver's seat in the 115-degree heat?

It gets worse. Not only does Yuma (which I believe is Spanish for "the dog just burst into flames on the patio") have better weather than Honolulu, but so do Las Vegas, Phoenix, El Paso, Albuquerque and San Diego.

That's according to a list of the 10 best weather cities in the United States published by the *Farmers' Almanac*. Amazingly, Honolulu is not even on the list. Considering that, you might honestly ask yourself, what in the hell are those farmers smoking? But it gets even worse. The magazine also published a list of the worst weather cities in the country and green, moist Hilo, that charming little Big Island town, was on that list.

Hilo, which admittedly has a rainy disposition, was lumped in with places like Astoria, Washington; Syracuse, New York; and Eugene, Oregon, as having the worst weather in the country. Please. Hilo's weather isn't even the worst in Hawai'i. Mt. Wai'ale'ale on Kaua'i is the wettest place on earth. It has something like 3,000 inches of rain a year. It's the only mountain in the world with a snorkeling concession on its peak. But to say Hilo's weather is as bad as Washington State's or Oregon's is sheer madness. Yes, it rains in Hilo. But it's *warm* rain. And it will rain for a few minutes in Hilo and then the sun will come out. In Eugene, Oregon, residents only see the sun two days out of the year. And then it's toweling off.

So I was shocked that Hawai'i's weather would be demeaned (twice!) by a little magazine that for 185 years has been a part of American history. The *Farmers' Almanac* is the periodical that generally makes eerily correct predictions about the weather a year in advance, theoretically based on the accumulated wisdom of farmers and weather-watchers across the country's heartland. It also contains recipes and offbeat stories of rural life, and declares in its most recent edition that apple pie really is "America's Dessert." So how could it be so far off on picking the best cities for weather?

I called the editor, Peter Greiger, who defended his best weather list. He said Yuma has sunny weather 90% of the year. Las Vegas and Reno have sunny weather more than 80%. And those cities also are the fastest-growing cities in the country. Honolulu only has sunshine 71% of the time.

I immediately figured out the problem. The man was confusing sunshine with good weather. Yes, it is sunny in Arizona and Nevada. But it's 145 degrees outside. It's so hot, you can fry an egg on a chicken stricken with heat stroke. You need a Bedouin camel driver just to take you to your car.

And I pointed out that rain does not necessarily mean bad weather. In Hawai'i, we actually enjoy the rain. People have outdoor weddings and, if it rains, they consider that a blessing.

"I live in Maine, so what do I know?" Greiger said. "But nobody ever asks, 'Where can I go where it's raining all the time?'"

Yeah, but nobody asks, "Where can I go where I'll need an air conditioner installed in my undershorts?" either.

And as for bad weather, Hilo's not even in the running. What's a little rain compared to a winter in Juneau, Alaska? In the winter there it's 80 degrees below zero, and you have to buy your sunlight in vacuum-packed cans. And why wasn't Fargo, North Dakota, on the Worst Weather list? Unlike Hilo, you never see an aloha shirt in Fargo in February. Did you ever wonder why Babe the Blue Ox is blue? He's freezing, man.

When it comes to weather, the less you have, the better. Hawai'i will always be at the top of that list, no matter what a few farmers say.

# More Bad News for Honolulu

T he good news is that residents of Honolulu don't drink as much alcohol as the boozers in San Jose, California, and Anchorage, Alaska. The bad news is we drink as much as they do in Passaic, New Jersey.

Bad, because while Honolulu has lots of cultural and recreational diversions, from surfing to the symphony, Passaic's a tiny city whose claims to fame are (according to Passaic's Internet Web site) a city hall that looks like a concrete missile bunker and that rubbish is picked up twice a week. If we're boozing it up as much as diversion-challenged Passaic residents, we need to get out of the house more.

I learned about our drinking problem and how Honolulu stacks up (or leans against) against other cities in categories such as "Most Dangerous Cities" in a newly released book called *The Definitive Guide to the Best and Worst of Everything*. I mean, newly released to the bargain book bin of a local bookstore. It actually was published a few years ago. But what it lacks in up-to-date statistics is certainly made up for by its $2.99 price tag.

Being easily agitated, I'm always keen to see how Honolulu is mistreated in this type of book. This one did not let me down. Honolulu did not even make the list of places in the world with the "most pleasant year-round weather." Casablanca and Mexico City did. Are they insane? I've been to Casablanca. Trust me, anywhere that is so freaking hot that you have to wear window draperies as clothes is not pleasant. And there is so much air pollution in Mexico City that no one there has even *seen* weather since 1966. But we should be used to this kind of disrespect. We were equally slighted recently by the *Farmers' Almanac*, which suggested that places like Las Vegas and Phoenix had better weather than Honolulu, which I suppose they do if you are a cactus.

The "best and worst" book listed the Honolulu-to-Kahului, Maui, airline route as the eighth busiest in the country, with more than 2 million people a year making that trip. I'm not sure if that's good or bad. It didn't include the Maui-to-Honolulu flight route, so I guess that means Maui now has about 90 million people living there.

We were listed No. 1 in the "Highest Home Costs" category, which is always a strong event for us. Strangely, we're also listed as having the lowest property tax rates in the country, which apparently drove our lawmakers to wonder, "How did we ever let that happen!?" I think our property tax rates have more than caught up by now. My wife opened our recent property tax assessment and passed out. When she regained consciousness, she said we were moving to Liberia, where you are legally allowed to shoot anyone who is involved in the tax-assessment business.

Honolulu thankfully was not listed among cities with the highest murder rates, greatest snowfall and most indicted public officials. (If the last one had been *newest* indicted public figures, I'm pretty sure we would have been in the running.)

The reason Honolulu always does so badly in these kinds of books and studies is that we let other people write them. We need to conduct our own research, with categories in which we excel. I'm sure Honolulu would be tops in the category of "Cities Where Women Wear the Most Gold Bracelets on One Arm" or "Cities Where the Word Pūpū Is a Good Thing." And we'd certainly win in "Cities with No Daylight Savings Time."

And just to make sure people know the difference between having a cocktail in Passaic and having one in Honolulu, we'd have a category called "Cities Where You're Most Likely to Find Fruit and Paper Umbrellas in Your Drinks." We might even beat Las Vegas on that one.

# The Gods Weren't Crazy about Tantalus

I'm sure a lot of nice people live on Mount Tantalus, that lovely peak towering above Honolulu and Pearl Harbor. But I've always detected a hint of smugness among the inhabitants of that lofty perch, as if they were Greek gods looking down on the rest of us.

It turns out the god thing isn't just a coincidence. I recently discovered that our Mount Tantalus shares a connection to the mythical gods of Mount Olympus, but not in a way that brings any credit to the owners of the million-dollar homes that boast breathtaking views from Diamond Head to Barbers Point.

In fact, if Tantalus residents knew the true story of their mountain's namesake, it might wipe the smugness off their faces, or at least make them claim that they thought Tantalus was named after "the third paddler on the right in the first Polynesian sailing canoe to land in the Islands."

I came across the real story of Tantalus while doing some light reading (as I'm apt to do) in a delicate 12-pound volume of ancient Greek mythology. (You ought to see my heavy reading.)

To put it lightly, this guy Tantalus was a real piece of work.

First of all, he wasn't a god, as some references to Tantalus in Hawai'i housing, hiking and travel brochures allege. Although he was the son of Zeus, the father of all the gods, he was a mortal. He was the king of Sipylus and extremely rich.

He was sometimes allowed to join Zeus and the gods on Olympus at meals, but he made a real pig of himself, scarfing down nectar and ambrosia. It's said that he even stole some of the nectar and ambrosia to share with his mortal friends, which was stupid because, even for the gods, ambrosia didn't come cheap.

He also eavesdropped on the immortals' conversations and then told all of his mortal friends what they said. That was not such a big deal, because what the gods usually talked about was how freakin' expensive ambrosia was and why was it so hard to get your immortal hands on a good bottle of vintage nectar nowadays?

Tantalus apparently was something of an arrogant jerk who didn't believe the gods really had all the power they claimed to have. So, as we'll see, he kind of screwed up there.

Just to act like a big shot, Tantalus invited the gods to dine in his palace. And to discover if they were really all knowing, he prepared an interesting test: he had his own son, Pelops, slain and turned into stew for the gods' dinner. It wasn't what you would call an "Olive Garden moment."

Well, most of the gods knew immediately something was up. The fact that the odd femur and skull were floating around in the cauldron might have been a clue. Greek mythological history says that only Demeter, who wasn't the sharpest arrow in the gods' quiver, "ate of the gruesome dish," munching happily on an entire shoulder blade. (She later reported it tasted like unicorn.)

The other gods threw the pieces of Pelops back into the cauldron, and Clotho, one of the fates (the showoff one), resurrected Pelops, with an ivory shoulder to replace the one that Demeter ate. (Things were a bit tense between Demeter and Pelops after that.) For his little stunt, the gods sent Tantalus to Hades, where he was forced to stand for all eternity in a lake whose waters came just to his chin. It was Hades, so you know it was pretty hot. But whenever Tantalus dipped his head to drink water, the water would recede. I don't know about you, but as a punishment from the gods, I think this was a pretty good one. There also was apparently some delicious fruit trees that the gods put just out of Tantalus's reach, so he was kind of bumming there, too.

Now, our Mount Tantalus was allegedly named by some hiking students who thought they were naming it after "a Greek god who was always thirsty." Yeah, he was thirsty. And roasting in Hades for all eternity. Not exactly the kind of guy you want to be naming large scenic wonders after.

The story of Tantalus actually gets worse. He had a daughter, Niobe, the queen of Thebes, who ticked off another god. That god had Niobe's seven daughters and seven sons killed in front of her and then turned Niobe into a block of marble. (The gods had very little sense of humor in those days.)

So, those residents of our Mount Tantalus should consider

being a little more humble as they sit on their mountain and look down on the rest of us mere mortals of average real estate. You might have a great view, but your dude, Tantalus, was a real idiot.

# A Used Lei Can Still Bring Joy

What do you do with a used lei? I don't mean one that has gone completely limp and dried out, but one that still looks decent and smells good.

It's impossible to just throw a lei away. It seems, well, unseemly. Even after a birthday or graduation, when you have mounds of leis, you can't just toss them in the Dumpster. There's nothing sadder than a lei in a Dumpster. Unless it's a street person wearing a lei in a Dumpster.

The most difficult type of lei to recycle is the one I call the "George Ariyoshi Lei." George Ariyoshi was governor of Hawai'i for many years, the first Asian American to become a governor of a state. For some reason, Ariyoshi seemed fond of the huge, red double-carnation leis. Huge leis. He wore so many I think he had a permanent double slump in his shoulders.

The average double-carnation lei weighs 43 pounds. And no matter how much you shake it, four quarts of water stay hidden in its petals. So not only do you feel like you are carrying a piano on your back when you wear one, you also get soaked.

The double-carnation lei is the one you want to get rid of first because it cuts off circulation to your lower body. But what do you do with them? They are too big to hang on your car's rearview mirror, a usual place for used leis. You hang a double-carnation lei on your rearview mirror and you might as well drive backward, because the rear view is all you are going to see. The lei will block your entire front windshield.

A double carnation is perfect to hang on the bow of a battleship, but you usually don't have one of those sitting around the house. The lei also comes in handy if you have a winning Kentucky Derby horse in your backyard.

You could hang one around the neck of the Kamehameha statue in front of the Supreme Court building, but then all the tourists would wonder why a statue of George Ariyoshi is standing out there.

When it gets right down to it, the only thing to do with a used double-carnation lei is to surprise total strangers, preferably from Ohio, and put it around their necks. They will think it is charming and walk around Waikīkī beaming, until they realize they are losing feeling in their fingers.

Most leis are easy to recycle, especially the lighter ones. Dogs like to get leftover leis. They don't understand them, but they like to get them. They'll run around the house and act goofy and pose for photographs with leis around their necks. Then they'll chew them up and leave the flowers scattered all over the place.

But never, ever try to lei a cat. Try to put flowers around a cat's neck and he'll take your arm off.

You can drape leftover leis over just about anything and they'll make that spot seem special. Dressers, doorknobs, mirrors, unused exercise equipment...it's like spreading colorful little exclamation points around the house.

The problem for most of us is not how to get rid of a used lei, but how to get lei'd to begin with. I usually get a lei when asked to speak to various community groups. But you can only give so many bad speeches before word gets around and your lei supply dries up. When I am presented with a lei during an event, I usually deliver it to my wife. She likes to wear leis, except the George Ariyoshi kind. She says she doesn't have the upper-body strength for them. She usually wears the lei to work the next day and her girl friends think, mistakenly, that I'm some kind of a great guy. Then she brings it home and hangs it on a shelf on the wall that has several pegs for hanging hats. We have no hats, but the pegs are perfect for hanging used leis. That's the cool thing about leis, they grow old gracefully, putting out a nice scent and actually looking better as they dry out, unlike husbands.

# Power Supply Supported by Termite Food

It's hard to understand the surprise when a bunch of wooden power poles fall down. After all, consider the fact that we're essentially supporting Hawai'i's power grid on large stalks of termite food that we then pound into the ground so the bugs can get at them easier.

To put it in another perspective, think of telephone and power poles as giant, glorified Slim Jims and termites as tiny little ground sharks. Yum, yum.

I don't care what you coat the wooden poles with; they are still termite food, and termites are going to find a way to hold their little noses, chew past the yucky protective coating and get at that delicious timber. And after they've gorged themselves the timber is going to go TIMBER! and fall over. Which is what happened not long ago in Wai'anae, the rustic community on the dry Leeward side of O'ahu. Several telephone poles toppled like dominos, blocking the only highway in and out of the west side for hours.

Officials said they are investigating the power poles to find out exactly why they fell, but trust me here, they didn't fall because they suddenly got bored with life. Or because of the Earth's magnetic pull. Or because an anti-electric-power nut secretly cut them down to protest global warming.

They fell because when you stick large pieces of wood in the ground in a tropical environment, termites eat them, or they rot, or both. And then a mild breeze finishes the job. They fell because we are using 19th-century technology to support 21st-century power and communications conduits.

Hawai'i's power and telephone poles aren't much different from the ones first put up to string telegraph lines through the West during Wild Bill Hickok's days. That technology made the venerable Pony Express obsolete, and yet, in 150 years, we haven't figured out a way to kill the obsolete telephone pole industry.

We *could* replace all wooden poles with metal ones, but then

O'ahu would look like Frankenstein's laboratory. The point is not to make Island eyesores more impregnable, but to get rid of the buggers altogether.

It's clear the only way to improve the views and electrical and phone service is to bury these stupid cables. We have the technology. It was developed even before Wild Bill Hickok and the telegraph. It's called *digging*.

Bury the cables in termite-proof space-age composite tubes and let the termites go back to eating our houses like they are supposed to. We live in the future. Let's act like it.

# Dumping on the Rubbish Cans

I was all ready to rage against the city paying $773 apiece for rubbish cans in Waikīkī until I actually saw one of the things and thought, you know, for a trash can, it's a fairly handsome object. And you have to remember, everything's expensive in Waikīkī: hamburgers, Mai Tais, prostitutes. You don't want your trash cans to have some sort of inferiority complex. A Waikīkī trash can holding the wrappers for $10 burgers and standing just a few feet away from $500 streetwalkers needs to exude a little dignity. And these new garbage cans do. They stand along Waikīkī's new wide brick sidewalks like proud little sentinels, or as proud as sentinels can be when filled to the brim with rubbish.

They are designed with slats to deter graffiti and built for the heavy duty of storing the upscale international trash that Waikīkī attracts (and we aren't talking visitors).

As anti-graffiti features go, the slat design is passive and friendly. I suppose that for a little more money the city could have purchased the more aggressive anti-graffiti rubbish cans which, upon sensing spray paint or permanent marker being applied to their epidermis, cause a small automatic weapon to emerge, which cuts down the offenders as if they were in a Charles Bronson movie. That would be overkill. At least for a tourist-related rubbish can. So even though these $773 receptacles have been derisively referred to by critics as "the Cadillacs of trash cans," we're lucky the city didn't spring for the Hummer version.

And about that cost, $773 per can, is it really that much? Those ugly gray and blue brutes that the city has installed in front of every home probably cost a couple of hundred bucks each. They are a blight on our Island views, and not only do they not deter graffiti, they seem to encourage it. By their owners. Technically, the city owns these trashcans that enable a rubbish truck driver to empty them without leaving the driver's seat. But many residents, apparently afraid that their neighbors are going to steal their personally assigned eyesores, spray-paint their names, addresses and astrological signs all over the sides of the repugnant receptacles.

I doubt you could find a decent heavy-duty trash can at the hardware store for less than $100, and none that could stand up to a minute-by-minute onslaught by trash-wielding tourists. And when you consider some of the other outlandish ways our tax money has been spent, these trashcans seem like quite a deal.

A big fan of the new cans, Don Poole, put it this way: "Let's start off reminding everyone that we built a stadium near the ocean that was expected to rust, and it did. We bought a sophisticated barge to clean our boat harbors; it never did. We built a softball field at the University of Hawai'i in which the fans in the stands could not even see home plate. We purchased an automatic pothole fixer that never fixed a pothole. We built a Visitors' Center at Hanauma Bay that blocked the view of Hanauma Bay. So why the controversy about well-made trash receptacles built with slats so that wind can pass through them and not knock them over and graffiti cannot be applied? They look good and they work."

As much as I enjoy dumping on the way city officials usually spend our tax money, I agree with Don. At least this money went *for* deluxe rubbish cans instead of *inside* them.

# The $10,000 Hole

M ike Leary is one of those guys you have to envy. His job is tearing things down. He's a demolition man. How great would it be to wake up knowing that you get to go out and demolish something? And get paid for it. He's demolished more than half the stores at legendary Ala Moana Shopping Center so people could put in new stores. He's demolished chunks of hospitals and schools. Anything needs tearing down, Mike's your man.

But his most memorable job wasn't knocking down a building. It was drilling a one-inch hole. A one-inch hole that cost taxpayers $10,000.

As head of Island Demo, Inc., Mike's learned that being a demo man isn't as easy as it used to be. To be a demo man today, you have to be part scientist, part safety engineer, part evacuation specialist and part hazardous waste expert. But he didn't think he'd need to wear all those hats to drill a one-inch hole.

The adventure in bureaucracy began when he sent one of his estimators to scope out a federal government project that had been put out to bid. (Mike won't say where this project was because he still has to make a living in this town.)

What was needed was a one-inch-diameter hole through a concrete block wall so that a computer or electrical cable could be fed through. Mike thought the job might go for $200. Max. His estimator laughed. When Mike went to the first meeting about the project, he found out why.

He was amazed to find 12 people at the meeting. Why? Because the project involved a small amount of asbestos and lead paint, he said.

According to an account of the meeting Mike gave in a building industry magazine, there were three engineers, a project manager, two quality assurance inspectors, one safety officer, an Environmental Protection Agency compliance manager, two industrial hygienists and two administrative contracting officers. He was questioned about everything from a health and safety plan to a decontamination shower, from where the waste from the one-inch hole would be shipped to whether he had a respiratory-protection program, fire-escape plan and air-monitoring plan.

The most outrageous aspect of the project was that none of these precautions was mandated by federal law. They were put in the contract, Mike said, because the administrators "didn't want to take any chances."

"I left the meeting thinking, wow! A $200 hole in the wall escalated to $10,000 for the sake of regulation. So that's where a chunk of my hard-earned tax dollars is being thrown away," he said in his magazine piece.

It didn't even matter that the money was going to his company.

"It's nice that we get some of it, but that's not the point," Mike told me. "How much more craziness is there going to be?"

Island Demo got the contract. It took him an entire day to "encapsulate the area" to create a "negative air" space so that no lead or asbestos would escape. How long did it take to drill the hole?

"Fifteen minutes," he said.

For the demolition man, it was 15 minutes he'll never forget.

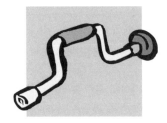

# Aloha from Hawai'i!
# Wish You Were Here (and Not Me!)

*Newspaper Headline: "Horrible Weather Continues to Smash
Islands; Officials Say It Hasn't Hurt Tourism Yet"*

Dear Mom and Dad,

Aloha from Hawai'i! I just wanted to thank you for allowing me
to come to the Islands for Spring Break! I feel a little guilty leaving
you back there on the mainland with the snowstorms and everything.
Brrrrrr!

I've got a great hotel room overlooking Waikīkī Beach! It
looks fabulous! At least, the scenes of Waikīkī Beach on the hotel
TV's visitor channel look fabulous. It's been raining since I landed.
I can't quite make out the beach from my patio through the drizzle.
I'm told Diamond Head is just over there, at about 3 o'clock as the
pigeon flies. Can't wait to see it!

My friends and I planned to go shopping later today, but the
main drag through Waikīkī, Kalākaua Avenue, has been closed off.
Apparently a sewer line broke and is spewing you-know-what all over
the place! Just like home! But the local news says they've got it under
control and are pumping the untreated poo-poo into a lovely canal
near the hotel where we were going to go canoe paddling tomorrow.
Guess that's off, hee-hee!

Our surfing lessons also are going to have to wait. That canal
apparently feeds into the ocean and, well, the surf spots are all yucky-
poo. But that's all right. I'm not sure I want to surf anyway. Did I
mention a girl surfer was attacked by a shark yesterday? She didn't get
killed or anything. Just a bite on the leg. She looked pretty cheerful
on the news for someone attached by a large marine predator. They
are keeping her in the hospital to make sure she doesn't have rabies or
something.

The mountains looked really green when we were flying in.
Can't wait to see them up close. The hotel concierge said he will tell

us as soon as Civil Defense thinks the landslides have stopped. In the meantime, we may go hiking inside a nearby mall.

The local people here consider this pretty bad weather. Ha! They don't know bad weather! Wait a sec. A reservoir just burst on Kaua'i and flooded a neighborhood, dragging several people into the sea. Well, that's pretty bad weather. They say more of these little dirt dams all over Kaua'i could burst at any minute. Guess we'll mark that island off our itinerary!

I would rather go to the Big Island anyway. Can't wait to see a real volcano! Uh oh. A news alert just said that Mauna Kea has been closed because of a huge snowstorm. Snow? In Hawai'i? Is that allowed? I came here to get away from snow. Is it following me? This is weird.

Room service just knocked. Hey, they delivered some pineapples and several large bottles of liquor. Said it was a gift from the Hawai'i Visitors' Bureau. It's got a sympathy card attached! How funny! Before he left, the room service guy pointed out a waterspout out in the ocean. Through the rain clouds I could see it. A waterspout is like a tornado but it's not a real tornado because it's in the ocean. Pretty neat looking, like a big swirling bowl of water 100 feet high. It's coming toward the shore. Okay. It's a tornado now. There goes the surfboard racks. Sheesh, we don't even have tornados at home!

I'm on my third Mai Tai now. I think it's a Mai Tai. I just mixed a little from every bottle they sent up and stuck a stalk of pineapple in it. I'm watching an old *Magnum P.I.* on TV. Pretty neat! Wish I could have stayed at Magnum's house. Looks pretty sunny. Cheers, Thomas Magnum. Great paradise you got here. What, no sleet? Where's the hail? Oh, there it is. Out on the lānai. Perfect size chunks for my drink, though.

A seagull just flew into the sliding glass door. I think it committed suicide.

I know how he's feeling. I could have gone to Aruba. It might not be the safest place for young women travelers, but at least you can go outside. Haiti might have been nice.

Hold on. Good news! Weatherman says the trade winds are returning and the rain will stop tomorrow. Hooray! The hurricane isn't expected to hit until Friday.

Love and kisses and aloha from Hawai'i! Wish you were here. And not me. I'll never forgive you for ruining my Spring Break.

Your slightly inebriated daughter,
Bethany

# The Trouble with Tourism: Tourists

It's hard to believe that in a state whose livelihood is based on tourism, some people want to get rid of the tourists. The Sierra Club actually demanded a study be done to figure out the harmful effects all these pesky tourists have on Hawai'i's environment.

You could call the Sierra Club a bunch of self-appointed busybodies who don't understand that tourists actually are good for Hawai'i, but you'd have to conduct an environmental impact study to determine the detrimental effects your words might have on the Sierra Club's internal egosystem. The Sierra Club actually sued the state to block the Hawaii Tourism Authority's madcap plans to try to get more tourists to come here. It may not be enough. We may have to meet the tourists on the airport tarmac and beat them back on the plane with baseball bats.

Or at least detain tourists when they get off the plane and ask them just what their greedy, environment-destroying plans are for our precious state. I picture a Hawai'i Tourism Environmental Impact Strike Force agent pushing a tourist against the wall at the baggage claim area.

**Agent:** Drop the bag, punk. What's that around your neck?

**Tourist:** A plumeria lei. Someone just gave it to me.

**Agent:** A lei, eh? So, you're already raping our plumeria trees. Do you know the impact of millions of tourists on our precious trees? There are flowers being savagely ripped off just so you can wear them around your haole white neck.

**Tourist:** Uh, no.

**Agent:** Well, it's bad. Now, what do you plan to do while you're here?

**Tourist:** Just go to the beach, play golf...maybe hike a little bit. The usual tourist stuff.

**Agent:** Usual tourist stuff, eh? You scumbag. You'll slather yourself up with sunblock and then get in the ocean, putting out an oil slick. Multiply that by a coupla thousand and you got an Exxon

Valdez crashing into Waikīkī Beach.

**Tourist:** What if we just sightsee?

**Agent:** I suppose you'll want to rent a car?

**Tourist:** Sure.

**Agent:** Sure! Put one more car on our already overcrowded highways. One more car spewing exhaust into our precious air. You have a few days of fun while the people of our state are left gagging.

**Tourist:** We'll take the bus.

**Agent:** Ha! That's worse. Tourists hogging all the seats on the bus so that our citizens can't get to their jobs and the economy is ruined.

**Tourist:** How about if we walk?

**Agent:** You are slime, aren't you? What, you never heard of ants? Do you know how many ants you're gonna kill walking around on our precious sidewalks? Not to mention cockroaches and centipedes. They have a right to life, too, you murderer.

**Tourist:** What if we just stay at the hotel and play golf?

**Agent:** Do you have any idea what the chemical run-off from golf courses does to our precious water supply? We've got kids with three heads being born next to golf courses.

**Tourist:** We'll stay in the room and order room service.

**Agent:** Sure, and have the air conditioner cranked up to the max while your lānai door is wide open. You know what the blast of cold air does to flying insects trying to survive in the hotel lānai ecosystem? We have more endangered insect species than anywhere on Earth. One blast of cold air and you could wipe out the entire gene line of two or three species.

**Tourist:** OK. You win. We're going home right now. Mind if we just sit over there until the plane is turned around? We won't do anything but breathe.

**Agent:** Breathe? Now you want to BREATHE our air? Do you know what happens when all you selfish tourists BREATHE OUR AIR? You put foreign germs in our precious air space!

# Hey Waiter, There's An Umbrella in My Drink!

I don't get into Waikīkī much. Mainly because it scares me. Surrounded by the Ala Wai Canal on three sides and fronting the ocean, Waikīkī is an island unto itself. Crossing into Waikīkī is like crossing into strange, dangerous territory. Oahu residents regard Waikīkī the way the people of Albania regard Montenegro. Or the way people of Slovenia regard Croatia. Or the way the United Arab Emirates regard Michael Jackson. That is to say with fascination, tempered by suspicion and a healthy bit of paranoia.

The people in Waikīkī dress in clothes whose garish colors appear on no normal color chart. They pay money to have large birds the color of their shirts and muʻumuʻus pose on their shoulders. Kalākaua Avenue smells like coconut—coconut sunscreen. Tourists fresh off the plane from places on the mainland that get no sunlight are said to burst into flames the first time they go to the beach. The City & County of Honolulu has guys in Hazmat suits patrolling the beaches with fire extinguishers to put out the flaming tourists. Currency, whether it be American dollars, Japanese yen or Euros, loses 50 percent of its value when it is transported over the Ala Wai bridge into Waikīkī. The food is good in Waikīkī but they do weird things to it. The fish is burnt on the outside and left raw on the inside. Why? Perfectly good New York steaks are saturated in teriyaki sauce. Pineapple is routinely put on pizza, which I think goes against the Geneva Convention. And bartenders put foreign objects into your drinks for no apparent reason.

I recently went against my better judgment and conducted a reconnaissance mission into Waikīkī. It had been years since I ventured into the so-called "concrete jungle." I wore triple-strength radiation-blocking sunglasses, not just to appear incognito but to protect my eyeballs against the damaging rays bouncing off the aforementioned aloha shirts and muʻumuʻus. If you happened to look directly at a family of five wearing identical cosmic red, orange and yellow aloha attire, you would go blind.

Here are some of my field notes from my incursion
into Waikīkī:

- Forget the Mai Tai. There are now 2,543 different exotic
drinks available in Waikīkī with names like Sex on a Surfboard While Dropping Into a Gnarly Right-hander, the
Miranda Warning, the Super-cala-fraja-listic-expi-Haole-rita
and the strangely named Wilbur, a coma-inducing alcoholic
concoction poured into a hollowed-out pineapple and set
ablaze with a road flare. Despite the advanced mixological
nature of these cocktails, they still come adorned with a paper
umbrella, vintage 1954. You'd think that in the 21st century they'd have a more technologically advanced method of
protecting an exotic drink from the harmful rays of the sun
than a paper umbrella. Who decided that certain alcoholic
beverages need to be protected with umbrellas, anyway? I've
never seen a drink get sunstroke. And it's not just umbrellas
they stick in your drinks. Pineapple stalks, chunks of oranges,
handfuls of cherries, curlicue straws (which, if untangled,
would reach to Moloka'i), olives, onions, limes, kiwi fruit,
mangos, papayas, bamboo reeds—you need a machete to chop
your way to the liquid part of the drink.
- Limousines are now officially the longest vehicles on the
planet. I saw one white limo that stretched from Fort DeRussy
to the Royal Hawaiian Hotel. You apparently board the
limo in the rear and are transported toward the front of the
vehicle by a set of pulleys and a trolley seat. You get out of the
front door and find yourself in a completely different area of
Waikīkī with the limousine itself never leaving the curb. A
stretch Hummer limousine offers the same service, but you
and your spouse enter the truck wearing matching aloha attire
and exit out the front 20 minutes later in battlefield
fatigues and Kevlar vests.
- The price of shrimp in Waikīkī apparently is tied by a legisla-
tive "shrimp cap" to the price of shrimp in selected shrimp-
producing regions such as Lawrence, Kansas, Irkutsk and
Burkina Faso (formerly Upper Volta). Ordering a single
shrimp at an outdoor café causes visitors at neighboring tables

to stand and applaud, camera flashes to light up the sky and a certificate of appreciation to be delivered to your table by a representative of the Hawai'i Visitors and Convention Bureau. A financially well-heeled tourist on one hotel floor apparently ordered an entire shrimp cocktail via room service, which caused the floor to be locked down by a fully armed SWAT team while the precious seafood was delivered. It was whispered that the gratuity from that order alone could have bankrupted a small country (like Burkina Faso).

• There is an ABC Store every three feet or so in Waikīkī. ABC Stores began as simple mini-markets where tourists could buy staples like beer and potato chips at reasonable prices ("reasonable" meaning reasonable to people in the more deserted parts of Antarctica than in a major tourist destination). ABC Stores flourished because tourists hate to leave Waikīkī almost more than Honolulu residents hate to enter there. ABC Stores eventually began to sprout on every street corner in Waikīkī but now have basically taken over the place. There is a movement to change the name of Waikīkī to ABC Store. Don Ho has an entire portion of his show dedicated to ABC Stores with such stirring island tunes as "Tiny ABC Stores," "The ABC Store Wedding Song," "One ABC Store, Two ABC Store," "I'll Remember ABC Store," "Blue ABC Store" and "Pearly ABC Stores."

• People used to be content to sit on famous Waikīkī Beach and listen to their sun blisters sizzle and pop. Now they want excitement. There are many death-defying things to do in Waikīkī, drinking a flaming pineapple drink and refusing to tip the bellhop being just a few. You can pay to be dragged behind a boat. Really. They'll even attach you to a parachute so you can be in the air while being dragged behind a boat. Whatever happened to just sitting in a boat? Another dangerous thing you can do is rent a detached airplane wing and try to catch waves on it. These airplane wings are about 30 feet in length and go by the not-so-subtle name "long boards." You will never catch a wave on one of these boards. But you will run into local chaps surfing on "short boards" who will pound you into poi for getting in their way. Another crazy thing to do in Waikīkī is to rent a gigantic floating tricycle. You can peddle these things on top of the water and go way out in the ocean where the Coast Guard won't find you. Or you can peddle in the way of a speeding boat dragging a tourist in a parachute behind it. And the inter-Island supply barges are fun to look at close up from a water tricycle, also. If you see one, it means you have drifted almost to Moloka'i.

So, that's my report on Waikīkī. Speaking of death defying, I had to flee for my life after I was unmasked as a Hawai'i resident interloper in Waikīkī. I was wearing my sunglasses and a red and purple mu'umu'u but I still got nabbed. It was right after I let my guard down and complained, "Hey waiter, there's an umbrella in my drink!" That blew my cover and I was forced to swim across the Ala Wai Canal at night. Luckily, the light from 14 ABC Stores lit my way.

two
———
# Critters in Paradise

*"We are alone, absolutely alone on this chance planet; and,*
*amid all the forms of life that surround us, not one, excepting the dog,*
*has made an alliance with us."*
—Maurice Maeterlinck

From frogs the size of pennies to centipedes the size of yard rakes, Hawai'i has more than its fair share of critters, most of them from someplace else. The coqui frog, our most recent immigrant, is the only species people want to wipe out because it is annoying. It emits a shrill chirp that has caused parsons to draw weapons. Other species, like the mongoose, have somehow endeared themselves to Hawai'i residents, even if, as is the case with the mongoose, they failed in their original mission to wipe out rats. It's well known that rats and mongooses often high-five each other coming and going from their various work shifts: mongooses off to hunt at night and rats off to hunt in the day. Or vice-versa. They toast each other at the local varmint bar, to the humans' confusion.

Mr. Maeterlinck's rather depressing observation nevertheless finds purchase in the Islands, where if you sit still long enough something will bite you. It probably won't be your dog, but there are plenty of other suspects to go around: mosquitoes, ants, scorpions, centipedes, wild boars and the occasional confused mynah bird. Most creatures in Hawai'i make no alliances, take no prisoners and grant no quarter (or dollar either). One thing they seem to have in common is that when they are inside, they want outside and when they are outside they want in. That includes your garage, your house and, alarmingly, your pants.

# How to Bug a Bug

One of the great things about living in Hawai'i is the variety of insect life. If you like bugs, you are in hog heaven. No. Wait. If you like hogs you'd be in hog heaven. I guess if you like bugs, you'd be in bug heaven. I don't think I'd like to go to bug heaven, even if I liked bugs. Okay. Forget all the heaven stuff. Hawai'i has a lot of bugs. So that's great if you like them. And it's even better if you like to kill them. People in Hawai'i have raised killing bugs to an art form. We've come up with many novel and interesting ways to dispatch the various multilegged critters and creepy-crawlies that share our homes in this tropical paradise.

Anyone can swat a cockroach with a rubber slipper or rolled-up newspaper, but it takes a real sportsman to pop the head off a roach with a blast of air from a hand-pumped target pellet pistol. No pellet is used, mind you, because if you miss your prey, you might take out a picture window or the neighbor's cat. You just pump the pistol with air, move the barrel within 10 inches of a free-range roach, and blammo!

Unlike when you go after a roach with a slipper, the big fella doesn't flee because he doesn't know what an air gun is. He just looks up at the barrel moving toward him, thinking, "Hey, now, what's this?" Before he can figure out he's in danger, you've Charlie Bronsoned him to…wherever bugs go when they're Charlie Bronsoned. Possibly bug heaven.

If you don't like to use bug sprays or other pesticides around the house, the lubricant WD-40 is a great way to dispatch all kinds of insects. WD-40 doesn't necessarily kill the little buggers right off, but they start running so fast they slam into a wall and conk themselves out.

And when you're dealing with one of those foot-long centipedes, remember that a small jackhammer is quite effective. I discovered this while jackhammering my hillside one day, when a centipede made the mistake of wandering by. He was quickly diced into several sections that proceeded to scamper in multiple directions with the intent, I think, of meeting and joining up later. While a jackhammer is a fun way to kill centipedes, your spouse will frown on your employing it inside the house.

My newest insect-control discovery involves using the spray-bottle kitchen cleaner Formula 409 to kill mosquitoes. This was a great breakthrough because it combines the thrill of the hunt with target shooting and housecleaning. If you miss the mosquito, which you will on your first few tries, you merely wipe the spray off whatever household appliance or piece of furniture you hit and—voilà—it's clean!

There is something in the formula of 409 that kills mosquitoes on contact. (I doubt that 409's predecessors—407 and 408—had this secret ingredient.) And like the air gun/cockroach dynamic, the mosquito doesn't flee for its life. He's looking for your hand or a fly swatter to be coming at him, not a big, friendly-looking bottle of 409.

When you get good enough, you can pick mosquitoes out of the air with a squirt of 409. I can't tell you how satisfying that is. It must be what World War I flying aces felt when then shot down an opponent.

You can also use 409 on roaches, but they tend to scurry behind couches or dressers to die. You'll find them—clean and shiny—later, lying on their backs in the "I'm a Goner" position. I always thought the way roaches turn over and die on their backs as one of their more charming features. It's really damn decent of them.

So, to recap: air guns for roaches, jackhammers for centipedes, 409 for mosquitoes and WD-40 for miscellaneous creatures. They are safe, fun ways to control pests, and relatively kind to the environment. I've been experimenting with trying to suck flies right out of the air and off tabletops with a vacuum cleaner nozzle, but early results aren't promising. So far I've caught pencils, potato chips and TV remote controls and scared the bejesus out of one of our love birds, pinning it to the inside of its cage.

At least I'm getting more housecleaning done.

# Those Randy Roaches

S*cience* magazine reports that researchers are close to coming up with a way to exterminate cockroaches based on the males' extraordinary sex drive. This is both good news and bad for Hawai'i, which boasts, not loudly or often, 19 species of cockroaches. The good news is that scientists are coming up with a way to kill cockroaches that does not involve rubber slippers or kayak paddles. The bad news is learning that male cockroaches are among the randiest disgusting insects in the world.

When the female cockroach squirts out a certain chemical pheromone, males will quit whatever they are doing (i.e. grooming your eyebrow while you sleep, scampering all over that apple you plan to eat in the morning, ganging up to mug smaller geckos in the corner of the garage) and run to get a little bit of hoochie-koochie.

Scientists have identified that pheromone and believe they can use it to trick male cockroaches into traps. Apparently the plan is to turn those "roach motels" into "roach brothels" where the males will enter thinking they are going to get some lovin' and end up getting a dose of a micro-organism that will eventually kill them. If you think that sounds suspiciously like what happens in the human world when a man goes into a house of questionable repute and engages in unprotected sexual congress (or even sexual executive branch) with tainted paramours, resulting in diseases best not discussed at the dinner table, if you think that…you're right.

"We hope it will be like a syphilis mode of insect control," said a Cornell University researcher.

The male cockroaches will meet up with their male buddies to brag about their sexual exploits, unknowingly passing the deadly germs to the other guys, kind of like really bad fraternity houses.

This seems to be a rather insensitive, not to mention, sinister, method of controlling cockroaches, to which I believe we can all say, "Bravo!" A Web site devoted to Hawai'i insects points out that cockroaches play an important role in the ecosystem by recycling dead vegetation. Ha. If that were true, then what are they doing in my bedroom, which, though a tad untidy, is conspicuously lacking in dead vegetation?

If boy roaches are going to jump every time a girl roach spritzes "come hither" juice in their direction, they deserve to catch something unpleasant, if not downright deadly. I hope this new love potion works, because I'd like to use my kayak paddle for what it was originally designed for: smashing centipedes.

# Crazy Ants

You'd think that if you lived on an island overrun with millions upon millions of land crabs the size of footballs—which have claws that can rip open a coconut and which once a year migrate en masse to the sea, climbing over hill, dale, house, car, baby and dog—you'd think that maybe those crabs were a problem.

You'd think that unless you live on Christmas Island off Australia, in which case you'd think that millions of crabs crawling all over creation is an amusing thing to see and that the heavily armed crustaceans bring a certain charm to an otherwise desolate coral speck in the ocean. I suppose when you live on an island named after a happy holiday like Christmas, you're apt to be a little more cheerful and tolerant of marauding entrees.

What the Christmas Islanders will not tolerate are ants, particularly the millions and millions of "Crazy Ants" which consider the millions and millions of land crabs food.

Crazy Ants are long-legged beasts that squirt acid to debilitate their prey and then swarm over them. Christmas Island, whose environment has been a delicate ecological balance of crabs, trees and people, has in recent years been thrown out of whack by Crazy Ants. The balance has shifted to become ants, crabs, ants, trees, ants, people, ants, ants and ants.

Nobody's sure why the Crazy Ants suddenly turned on the crabs, but scientists think it's either because they ran out of other species to fight (i.e., other ants) or that they're sick and tired of being called crazy. There is no end in sight to the mayhem the Crazy Ants are causing the crab population, which, though interesting in an Alfred Hitckcockian way, doesn't have anything to do with us in Hawai'i.

Or does it? It turns out that we have Crazy Ants here, along with 49 other species of ant. Thankfully, our Crazy Ants are so busy fighting with other ants for food and territory that they have been unable to turn their wrath on crabs, egrets, mynah birds, poodles or other moderate-sized creatures.

Crazy Ants are called that because they haven't mastered the most basic of ant skills, which is to say, walking in a line. But what they lack in line formation know-how, they make up in their ability to race around in complete chaos, terrorizing other life forms—preferably smaller than they are, but bigger is fine, too.

Along with Crazy Ants, Hawai'i has Carpenter Ants, Big-Headed Ants, Little Yellow Ants and Fire Ants. Those are honest-to-God names that scientists have given to ants. You never see ants called Friendly Ants, Comely Ants or Jolly Ants, which, to my non-scientific mind, may have something to do with why ants are so angry all the time.

So we have Crazy Ants, but they aren't really crazy, just kind of agitated. Hawai'i, in fact, has four of the eight most destructive alien species on the planet: Crazy Ants, mongooses, strawberry guavas and water hyacinths. We don't have four others: the Brown Tree Snake, the Nile Perch, the Zebra Mussel and the Bushtail Possum, though not for lack of trying. A couple of dead Brown Tree Snakes have been found at the airport on flights from Guam. If they do eventually get a foothold here, we can only hope our Crazy Ants find them tasty.

# Geckos Are Girls

I found out something amazing about geckos the other day. Get this: all geckos are paraplegic. Wait. That can't be right. That would mean that their back legs are paralyzed. How would they be able to cling upside down to the ceiling if they were paraplegic?

Let's see. It was par-something or other. Ah, I got it. All geckos are paradoxical. No, that's not it either. Although some geckos seem paradoxical. (Why would a creature spend his entire life hiding behind a picture on a wall and yet have no true appreciation of art?)

Maybe it was that all geckos in Hawai'i are Paraguayan? That doesn't make sense. How'd they get to Hawai'i? Did the Polynesians sail by South America in their canoes on their way to the Islands?

I can figure this out. A really smart guy told me this. A university professor. He said, all geckos in Hawai'i are par...par...par... parthenogenic! That's it! (It was just on the tip of my tongue. Actually, it's too big a word to be just on the tip of the tongue, it was sort of spread out in there, knocking up against the molars.)

Anyway, all geckos are parthenogenic. That means they are all females and don't need males to help them out in the reproductive department. Which is handy, since there are no males. I couldn't believe it when the professor told me that all geckos are chicks. You see them clinging to the screens, their translucent bellies stuffed with eggs, and you think, these babes must have been making hoochiekoochie. But no, they are able to lay fertilized eggs all by themselves.

I'm surprised feminists aren't all over this. Maybe there's a secret Gertrude Stein Gecko Parthenogenic Reproductive Research Center somewhere dedicated to finding out how geckos reproduce without males and then replicating that system in human females.

As a male, however, I find the idea that females, even if they are only lizards, can reproduce without the aid of a guy kind of depressing. Do girl geckos ever wish they could invite a male lizard of another species over for a couple of termites and then make out in the warm glow of a lānai light bulb?

I did a little research myself and discovered that my professor friend wasn't completely right. Not *all* geckos in Hawai'i are female and unisexual. There is one species of gecko that has both males and females. But the males are so big, strong and aggressive that they make life miserable for the females. I suspect those loud chirping sounds you hear in your bedroom at night are the pushy male geckos yelling to females to bring them the equivalent of gecko beers.

What all geckos do have in common are immovable eyelids and the ability to lick their eyes with their tongues. I guess that means that until the obnoxious males of that one species are dealt out of the evolutionary equation (no doubt coming soon) the females can lick away their tears.

# Toe Story

Geckos got fingers. Toes, too. And scientists have been wondering for decades exactly how those tiny digits work; how they allow the little buggers to walk along a ceiling as easy as crossing a tabletop.

In Hawai'i, we always knew geckos were special. We just didn't know that geckos, with their ability to defy gravity, were such serious targets of research.

Then I saw a wire-service story that said scientists at Lewis and Clark College in Portland, Oregon, have discovered that the gecko's clingability is not due to suction or stickiness, but to an electric reaction on a molecular level.

This should really embarrass Hawai'i's scientists in charge of studying little critters. We're busy fooling around with cloning green mice while scientists in some other state—a state that doesn't even *have* geckos—is snagging the national spotlight with important breakthroughs in gecko-related research. You probably can't even walk through a University of Hawai'i science lab without tripping over a gecko, yet none of our guys has bothered to figure out how gecko toes and fingers work.

And, this is important stuff. It may not be up there with the Big Bang Theory, but the gecko-ceiling suspension phenomenon is a real scientific mystery.

All the way back in 1923, naturalists were scratching their heads over it. In the book *Amphibia and Reptiles*, published by Cambridge University—*another* place that doesn't have geckos—the authors wrote: "The apparatus is complicated in its minute detail, but is very simple in principle. The adhesion is (not) effected by sticky matter but by small and numerous vacua." (Vacua are little suction thingies, sort of like microscopic toilet plungers.)

But the investigators back then really didn't understand the technology behind gecko suspension. "The more we ponder over the mechanism of their fingers and toes, the less we comprehend how such little vacua can support or suspend such heavy creatures from a dry and often porous surface," wrote the authors.

There's something kind of funny about people with important diplomas hanging on their walls, consumed with the toes and fingers of a bug-eyed lizard. But think about it: Wouldn't *you* like to be able to climb a wall or scamper across a ceiling?

That's part of the reason the Oregon scientists have been playing "this little piggy" with geckos. They want to develop synthetic gecko feet that could be used by search-and-rescue robots to climb walls. If they get that far, you can bet some entrepreneur will come up with gecko mitts for humans just for sport.

The way the Oregon brainiacs explain how gecko feet and hands work is really technical and difficult to understand. They do that on purpose. Basically, geckos have about a half-million tiny hairs on each foot and hand, and each hair has 1,000 tinier pads, smaller than the wavelength of light. They think some electric reaction occurs between these teeny pads that allows a gecko to support its entire weight with a single finger.

The researchers said a million of those hair-like fibers could fit on a dime and could lift a 45-pound child, which, you gotta admit, would be fun to watch.

We'd better get cracking if we are going to close the Gecko Gap. If anyone's going to hang from a ceiling with artificial gecko toes, it should be someone from Hawai'i.

# A New Lizard Slinks into Town

I recently received a tip from a highly placed imbiber of alcohol that there is a new lizard in town, and it lives on mosquitoes.

This happy news sent a shock wave through not only the Memminger Family Division of Lizards, which seldom unearths any exciting lizard-related information, but caused quite a stir among other family sub-entities, like the Department of Mongooses, Office of Plate Lunches and the highly regarded Cubicle of Chardonnay.

I had noticed that there didn't seem to be as many mosquitoes around this summer, and if a new mosquito-eating lizard is responsible, then God bless him. It wasn't long after hearing about the new lizard that I thought I saw one, a black-and-brown creature that marched across my living room carpet in broad daylight like he owned the joint.

It was startling because small reptiles in Hawai'i, like geckos, are usually seen darting along the walls, hiding behind picture frames. To see one hoofing it across the floor with no fear of foot, dog or vacuum cleaner was unnerving. My first thought was that if this little bugger lives on mosquitoes, he must be quite a jumper because mosquitoes don't generally hang out on the ground.

The Division of Lizards made inquiries to non-alcohol-imbibing sources to get the lowdown on this new lizard, only to learn that it is basically a myth.

A doctor at the state's Vector Control Branch has been conducting intense mosquito surveillance recently—not because he's weird and has nothing else to do, but because there's a danger that mosquitoes in Hawai'i might carry the West Nile virus. The West Nile virus is just as exotic and evil as it sounds, and if there was a lizard gobbling up mosquitoes, the Vector Control Branch would turn giddy. (The last time the Vector Control Branch turned giddy was when the Black Plague ended.)

Alas, word of the arrival of a new mosquito-eating lizard is an urban myth. Hawai'i's known geckos consider mosquitoes little more than aperitifs, and hard-to-catch ones at that. There are seven kinds of mosquitoes in Hawai'i, five of them blood-sucking. The other two types are on our side, brought to the islands in 1929 specifically to battle the bloodsuckers. Judging from the blood salad mosquitoes make of my legs on my lānai, our team doesn't seem to be winning the war.

Neil Reimer, manager of the State Plant Quarantine Branch, got my hopes up by saying that there is indeed a new lizard in town, but quickly dashed them by saying that town is Mānoa, the sleepy university suburb of Honolulu and miles from my side of the island.

Madagascar day geckos, brought here as pets, are now roaming the wilds of Mānoa but are not known as big mosquito eaters or little mosquito eaters, either. I saw a photo of a Madagascar day gecko, and he's pretty cute as far as geckos go. He's about seven inches long, green and scaly, with sinister red eyes—although, to be fair, the red eyes could have been the result of the camera flash. You know he's fast because he has orange racing stripes on the sides of his head.

Reimer says the lizard I saw in my living room was probably just a confused skink, looking for a pile of leaves to climb into, piles of dirty leaves being their favorite habitat. Skinks look exactly like lizards, but for some reason they got their name from furry tree-dwelling rodents that hang upside down by their prehensile tails. I suspect whoever was in charge of naming reptiles when skinks were discovered was in a lousy mood that day.

So, too bad. There's no new mosquito-eating lizard in town. But I did learn something important: when a skink strolls across your living room looking for piles of dirty leaves, it's probably time to vacuum the carpet.

# Worms on a Binge

O ne of the least known scientific facts in the whole world is that worms from Hawai'i hold their liquor better than worms from England.

I will give you a moment to recover from your surprise. There. Better? It is quite shocking to learn not only that worms drink, but also that worms from Hawai'i are world-class imbibers. We hear all the time about how our beaches and air quality are the best in the world, but the Hawai'i Visitors and Convention Bureau apparently has been keeping this whole boozing Hawai'i worm thing under wraps.

Actually, it's not really HVCB's fault. News of Hawai'i's drunken worms only was recently released in the widely read and immensely popular science magazine *Neuron*. (I know I run to the mailbox daily, eager to get the latest edition of *Neuron* in my mitts.)

In the June edition of *Neuron*, researchers disclosed that they had been testing the alcohol tolerance of worms because, well, somebody's gotta do it. I mean, do we really want to live in a world where drunken worms are sliming under the influence (SUI), careening around underground crashing into each other and nobody cares? At least, that's what I thought was going on until I got deeper into the story.

It turns out that worms—brace yourself—don't naturally drink alcohol. They basically have to be forced to do it. And you can't believe how hard it is to entice a worm into a bar and get him to have a couple of shots of Jack Daniels.

I don't really know how the scientists got the worms all liquored up. I'd use a tiny funnel or offer two-for-one specials, but I'm no scientist.

In any case, they get all these different worms drunk, and they discover that "Hawaiian worms" were more able to recover from intoxication than worms from England. Now, I don't believe there are any "Hawaiian worms" in Hawai'i any more than I believe there are "haole worms," "Portuguese worms" or "Chinese worms." Worms are worms. What the scientists meant was that these worms were "from" Hawai'i, worms that ended up in Hawai'i from somewhere else, sort of "kama'āina worms," if you will.

Our Island worms, apparently after a hard night of being force-fed tequila and Manhattans and singing "400 clods of dirt on the wall," sobered up faster than their English counterparts. They didn't throw up or anything. Maybe they did, but they're worms, so it was hard to tell. It could be throw-up, or it just could be, you know, regular old worm gunk.

Now we (finally) get to the reason getting Hawai'i worms drunk is important. It turns out that they have a certain gene that gives them a tolerance to alcohol. That gene might one day be spliced into human DNA to help cure alcoholism and make the patients long and skinny and excellent diggers.

Just kidding. It actually just helps scientists figure out why so many humans become alcoholics and how to cure them. So, next time you have a beer, say a toast to our slimy little buddies who are getting sloshed for mankind.

# Coqui Frogs on Caffeine

Ever since it was announced that caffeine would be used to kill off those hellishly noisy little coqui frogs that have invaded Hawai'i, I keep envisioning one of the frogs reaching up to a cashier at Starbucks for a double cappuccino latte and several of his friends pressing themselves up against the glass outside yelling, "No, Willy! Don't do it!"

I'm kind of surprised by the nearly universal blood lust against the tiny green creatures. As wildlife goes, they are cute little dickenses, about the size of a macadamia nut and able to leap over small buildings in a single hop. If track star Carl Lewis had been able to jump proportionately as far as a coqui frog, he would have been able to spring completely over four city buses and Rosanne Barr, which has almost nothing to do with what we are talking about here. But hopping is one of three things that coqui frogs do extremely well, which makes them hard to catch.

The second thing they do well is emit a loud, piercing screech or chirp, which scientists have measured on the same decibel level as a jet engine. The third thing they do well is make hoochie-koochie with each other, which is why there suddenly are so many of them in Hawai'i screaming up a storm. Put those three things together, and the coqui frog has the distinction of being the first animal species humans want to eradicate simply because it's annoying.

With so many endangered species in Hawai'i, more than anywhere else in the world, it only takes one foreign plant or animal to wipe out entire lines of life. If the brown tree snake got free in the Islands, it could wipe out most bird life, which would in turn wipe out many flowers and plants that depend on birds to propagate. The mongoose was brought in to kill rats, which it petulantly refuses to do, and now there are mongooses all over the place, turning over garbage cans and threatening animals smaller than they are. Kudzu vines invaded and now not only strangle native plants, but also cover telephones poles and abandoned cars, making them look like vegetable monsters.

There are all kinds of insects, animals and plants Hawai'i doesn't want, but the coqui is the only one on the hit list because it's noisy. It's too bad coqui frogs don't eat pests we hate, like those huge cockroaches and centipedes, but when you are the size of a macadamia nut, you have to pick your meals carefully.

So it's generally accepted the frogs have to go. Generally, but not unanimously. There are a few people in Hawai'i who used to live in Puerto Rico, where the coqui frog is revered. These people will tell you they love coqui frogs and that you get used to the chirps. Of course, these people's hearing is almost completely shot. ("Huh? Tell you about croquet hogs? I don't know any croquet hogs.")

Researchers have figured out that caffeine kills coqui frogs, which is surprising because you'd think it only stunted their growth. They discovered this apparently after trying all kinds of other harmful substances on the frogs: cigarettes, cheap white wine, fatty foods. Nicotine worked pretty well, but the tiny patches kept falling off. I'd have thought that alcohol would be effective at shutting the little buggers up. The moment one of them screamed on the morning after a coqui frog booze bender, the others would have killed him.

The researchers haven't decided exactly how to expose the frogs to caffeine. You can't just pump it out of helicopters into people's back yards. I think Starbucks holds the license on that. If the coqui frogs actually heard how much a cup of coffee costs these days, it might just leave them speechless.

# Frankenfish

A Texas company beat Hawai'i to the punch, coming up with a tropical household fish that glows in the dark. Hawai'i residents should be embarrassed. Hawai'i should be in the forefront of scientific breakthroughs involving anything in the fish line. We have more fish swimming around us than any state in the country, and if a fish is going to glow or do anything else helpful or amusing, it ought to be one of our fish.

The so-called GloFish actually were developed in Singapore by scientists who found they could turn the normally black-and-silver zebra fish green or red by inserting jellyfish or sea anemone genes.

The best Hawai'i scientists could come up with are genetically engineered green mice, whose marketing potential is limited to people who want mice, and green ones at that. Pink bunny rabbits would probably have been a better seller, especially at Easter. There might even be a market for purple nēnēs or chartreuse mongooses, something tourists might get a kick out of. But what did scientists at the University of Hawai'i develop? Green mice.

Glowing fish would be a natural, or an unnatural, actually, for Hawai'i. Imagine how much fun Hanauma Bay would be at night if filled with glowing fish.

It might be a good idea to develop glowing sharks so that they couldn't sneak up on surfers and swimmers at dusk or dawn. Genetically altering sharks so they don't have any teeth would make sense from a safety point of view, but environmentalists would whine that without their teeth, sharks would become the laughingstock of the sea world, bullied by bottom feeders and mollusks.

Environmentalists are already complaining about the glowing zebra fish. In California, detractors call them "Frankenfish" and don't want anything to do with them.

While the Texas company marketing the fish say they are safe, critics say there is no telling what would happen if the freaky fish got loose in the wild, as many aquarium fish do. They are a little vague about what dangers little glowing fish would pose if let loose, but I suppose their constant glowing could keep the other fish up at night and make them cranky and irritable.

Researchers claim that no harm comes from eating the glowing fish, a task that was likely forced upon the lowest and least-liked researcher on staff. ("OK, Professor Watkins has eaten 43 of the little buggers. Turn out the lights and let's see if he glows.")

Hawai'i scientists should immediately pursue research in the glowing fish field. Colored glowing sushi and sashimi could become a million-dollar industry for Honolulu.

And why stop there? What if Red Lobster restaurants actually offered red lobsters, glowing like firetruck strobes? What if you could get popcorn shrimp beaming like a bucket of Christmas lights? We are at the threshold of sitting down in a restaurant and being asked, "How do you want your ōpakapaka? Baked, sautéed or Day-Glo?"

# The Humu Is Hilarious in Scotland

One of my duties as a humor columnist apparently is to explain to people from other parts of the world some of the bizarre or purely silly things that happen in Hawai'i.

Which is why I once was interviewed on a radio show in Scotland attempting to justify why politicians here in the Islands have nothing better to do than argue over naming an official state fish.

It apparently was one of those *Animal House* radio shows with various zany DJs giggling to each other and making lewd double entendres and for some reason they really got a kick out of the *humuhumunukunukuapua'a.*

Maybe because it was midnight Hawai'i time (10 a.m. in Scotland) and I was half asleep that I didn't appreciate the extreme humor of the situation. Or maybe it was because it was like talking to three Mike Meyerses in full Shrek mode ("Aye, Donkey, watch oot for da hoo-moo-laki-laki-mooki-mooki fish! Hawhawhaw!")

To be fair, the guys seemed sincerely excited about speaking to someone from Hawai'i about a fish they had never heard of until they read about it on the news wire services. But that could have just been the whisky, which I think is considered a breakfast beverage in Scotland.

"This is a most peculiar story," said Fred MacAulay, host of the MacAulay & Co. morning show on BBC Radio Scotland.

I had been warned by a completely neutral associate of the program that it is "a hugely popular light-hearted, topical chat show that regularly plays host to top-named national and international celebrities."

Too bad. On this morning they were out of luck in the international celebrity category. They had a grumpy, sleepy unknown columnist half a world away.

"We're on an island and we don't have a state fish," said MacAulay, who's also a standup comedian. At least I think it was MacAulay. There was so much jabbering it could have been one of the other personalities—John Beattie, a former British Lions rugby star, or comedian Chris Neil. It's not that they all sounded alike, it's that they all sounded like Mike Meyers after a long Scottish breakfast.

I was pretty much inconsequential to the conversation as they took turns trying to pronounce *humuhumunukunukuapua'a*. and remarking that the little fish with the ridiculously long name probably goes well with "chips." (I think that's "French fries" for us, but it could have meant "poker chips" in Scotland for all I knew.)

I wanted to explain that the reason Scotland didn't need an official state fish is because it already had a largely hypothetical state monster that lives in Loch Ness. Why people who believe in a fictional lake beast would find Hawai'i's humuhumu so bizarre is hard to grasp.

Had the snickering and guffawing been less strident, I would have asked them about Scotland's official musical instrument, which seems to be a contraption made of a cow bladder, vacuum cleaner pipes and a wolverine with laryngitis.

I was able to tell them that opponents of the humuhumu in Hawai'i would rather have as the state fish the 'o'opu. Well, the comic possibilities of the word "'o'opu" were just too much for the crew, which collapsed into convulsive fits. You'd think they'd never heard of a fish name in which three out of four letters are vowels.

I felt a little uncomfortable sticking up for the humuhumu, considering I've often chastised our lawmakers for worrying more about naming a state fish than helping small business, housing the homeless or keeping the price of gas in Hawai'i lower than in Antarctica. But I felt it my patriotic duty to Hawai'i and its sea creatures to defend the humuhumu against bad puns and sarcastic remarks from people who consider deep-fried chocolate candy bars a treat. (Directions: Chill a Mars Bar, coat with batter, deep fry. Enjoy.)

Yes, it's a weird little fish with a long name, but it's ours, damn it. And if we want to have a state fish, a state insect or even a state household appliance, that's our business. Unlike Scotland, at least we know who wears the dresses around here.

# Box Jellyfish See Red

B ox jellyfish, those spineless lumps of gelatinous matter that
float to shore in Hawai'i every month and sting the living
bejesus out of anyone within tentacle reach, apparently hate
the color red. No kidding.

Australian scientists, for reasons yet unknown, decided to see
how box jellyfish react to certain colors and discovered the creatures
detest the color red. They found that when they placed a red object
into a tank with box jellyfish, the animals squirted hastily in the
opposite direction. This is considered a huge breakthrough in the
study of floating lumps of gelatinous matter, because if box jellyfish
hate the color red, they might have feelings about other things, like
Coke vs. Pepsi and the trouble in the Middle East.

The most immediate impact is that it could cause a major shift
in the color of swimming apparel. Red bikinis will be *hot* Down
Under this summer!

But it could have an impact in Hawai'i, too, because we have a
lot of box jellyfish. (Box jellyfish are so called because they are cube-
shaped, with four distinct sides. This is different from the 12-sided
polyhedron jellyfish, which often is so confused it doesn't know
which side is up.)

The problem is our box jellyfish are different from the box
jellyfish in Australia. The primary injury mechanism for all box jellyfish is stinging tentacles (although some have been known to carry
switchblades and spear guns). Our box jellyfish, the *Carybdea alata*,
impart a sting that is merely irritating, while the Australian variety,
the *Chrionex fleckeri* (also called "the sea wasp" and, behind its back,
"Bernard"), is a different story.

One jellyfish expert said this about sea wasps: "You have virtu-
ally no chance of surviving the venomous sting unless treated immediately. The pain is so excruciating and overwhelming that you would
most likely go into shock and drown before reaching the shore."

When you combine that with recent information that it hates

the color red, *Chrionex fleckeri* is a fairly unpleasant customer.

University of Hawai'i scientists need to begin conducting tests immediately to see if our box jellyfish dislike red and, more important, which colors they do like. If they are partial to chartreuse, for instance, you might want surf trunks of a different hue. Box jellyfish have about 37 eyes, so if they like a certain color and you are wearing it, dude, they're going to find you.

Another interesting thing about box jellyfish is that they have no heart. So when they sting you, they have absolutely no remorse.

They have no brain, either, but seem to have figured out how to come to shore the same time every month. They arrive en masse on O'ahu's South Shore nine to 10 days after the full moon, fully armed and ready to boogie. The City and County actually has a Web site with calendars showing when the slimy buggers are expected to show up. Signs also are posted when the box jellyfish arrive, so if someone is stupid enough to ignore the calendar and signs and get stung, they probably deserve it. (I've been stung many times, so I know what I'm talking about.)

If you do get stung, douse or spray the sting with vinegar. An old wives' tale suggests urinating on the sting, but I think that was just some old wives pulling someone's leg. On the other hand, it's unlikely that you'll have any vinegar with you at the beach, so you might as well try Plan B.

To recap: to avoid being stung by box jellyfish, check the government Web site, look for beach warning signs, wear a red wet suit and move to Las Vegas.

# Putting Teeth into Shark Management

I was shocked to find out that Hawai'i was dead last of all the Pacific states in shark management, mainly because I didn't even know that sharks had to be managed.

I always assumed sharks were the upper management of the ocean world, kicking butt wherever they saw fit. That included gnawing on the occasional swimmer, although I suspect that sharks enjoy chewing on people the way I would enjoy chewing on a raw shark fin.

But the National Audubon Society recently issued a report rating shark management in Hawai'i, Oregon, California, Alaska and Washington. Hawai'i got the worst score because of all the sharks killed around the Islands.

This just isn't fair. First of all, why is the Audubon Society worrying about sharks? Shouldn't it be taking care of birds? Maybe it can't attract as much in donations by issuing reports on lost parakeets as it can by issuing reports on sharks.

In the environmental world, sharks are sexy. They used to be considered ruthless predators that were better dead then fed. Now we are told that they actually are misunderstood gentle creatures who occasionally and inadvertently snatch a hapless sunbather off an inflatable raft because he or she resembles a turtle. It's cool to be concerned about sharks now, so the Audubon Society has forsaken its feathered friends for the bad boys of the deep.

Of course, the other Pacific states are going to look good when it comes to sharks because very few of their residents ever get eaten by one. You don't have a bunch of tourists chumming the water off Anchorage yelling, "Here, sharky sharky!" But in Hawai'i, thousands of potential sunburned meals bob around like a continual shark buffet.

But if shark management is as important as the Audubon Society says it is, I want to do my part. I've come up with a plan that will make Hawai'i's sharks the best-managed major ocean predators in the world.

First, if you are going to be a serious player in an enterprise involving the savage consumption of other species, you need a good public presence. A dynamic Internet site is the way to go. I picture one called killerfish.com that would give box scores in the sharks vs. humans competition. Sure, on paper, people are winning. People kill thousands of sharks per year. But sharks grab a lot more headlines. All a shark has to do is consume one important human, like a bishop or an underworld figure and, bam! He's on the front page.

After the Web site takes off, we will officially incorporate all of Hawai'i's sharks. We'll have a shark CEO and an entire shark board of directors. Then, we'll file a class-action lawsuit against all those fishermen who hack the fins off sharks and sell them for soup. With that money, we'll file with the Securities and Exchange Commission for an initial public offering. That's right, we'll sell stock. We'll launch our IPO on the Nasdaq, not the Dow, because the Nasdaq is where all the hot new predators hang out.

After several stock splits, we'll start preying on other shark companies, gobbling them up like they were guppies. In the end, we'll be a multi-oceanal conglomerate managing every shark on Earth.

The Audubon Society will rue the day that it accused Hawai'i sharks of being mismanaged. One day, killerfish.com will have the little birdie group for breakfast.

# Sign of Sharks

I guess if I were vacationing in Alaska and wanted to go on a hike, I'd appreciate it if the local authorities posted signs telling me on which trails I might encounter bears. It just makes sense to give visitors the choice between hiking on trails where large, heavily armed mammals are known to frequently drag people into the woods and trails that are generally bear-free.

So I didn't have a problem with Hawai'i's plan to post signs at one beach letting people know that that area of water is a known hangout for sharks and, historically, hungry ones.

The signs were to go up at Olowalu Beach on Maui, where there have been three shark attacks in 11 years. That actually doesn't seem like a lot of shark attacks when you do the math. It works out to about one shark attack every 1,500 days, so you are talking about sharks that aren't really taking their jobs seriously or who are moonlighting at other beaches.

I think tourists should know if certain beaches are favored by sharks. We put out signs warning people of dangerous waves and stinging jellyfish, so it makes sense to let them know a meat-eating predator may be in the water so they can decide whether they want to become food or not.

My problem was the passive wording on the proposed signs. The signs were to say: "Caution. Sharks May Be Present." Caution?

Caution is a word generally used when undertaking an enterprise in which you have the ability to protect yourself, like crossing the street or walking on a freshly mopped floor. You know that if you are cautious, if you wait until no cars are coming, you can cross the road in safety. Or if you tread carefully, you can walk across the wet spot on the floor without breaking your neck.

If there were a chance, however, that no matter how empty the road seemed, a deadly vehicle suddenly could come smashing through the pavement and swallow you whole, "caution" would not be the proper word of warning. "Danger!" would be the correct word.

"Watch Out! Very Weird Road!" might work.

Once you enter the ocean, it doesn't matter how cautious you are. If there is a hungry or belligerent shark in the vicinity, caution isn't going to save your butt. Being able to run across the surface of the water until you hit dry land is.

Likewise, the word "may" on the warning sign seems a little too soft for the occasion. "Sharks May Be Present" is way too passive. It's like saying the Earth *may* have been visited by extraterrestrials or you *may* have already won the Publishers Clearing House million-dollar drawing. "May" implies extremely long odds, bordering on impossible. In this case, people have seen the sharks at Olowalu Beach. They know they are there; they just aren't there this minute. There's a better chance you will see a shark at Olowalu Beach than Ed McMahon on your front porch.

I'm not sure what the wording should be. It doesn't have to be melodramatic, like warnings on medieval maps in sci-fi novels: "Here Be Dragons!" But it needs to have a little more oomph, like "Danger! Known Shark Area. Enter at your own risk. Condiments optional."

# Grooming Tips

The trouble with life is just when you think you've got it figured out, you learn something that shakes your entire belief system. Like, I just found out that Gillette Co., the folks who make shaving lotion and razors, used to use animals to test their products.

According to a Gillette official, the company no longer uses animals to test such products as Right Guard deodorant and White Rain shampoo.

But it still is shocking. Think of the long-term effects of teaching animals basic hygiene and then cutting them off. I can just imagine a bunch of animals sitting around in cages at the Gillette Testing Facility.

**Woodchuck 1:** Hey, Charley, I hate to be rude, but your deodorant just ain't cutting it these days.

**Woodchuck 2:** Oh, yeah, beaver-breath? Well, you're not exactly smelling like a field of posies yourself. It just so happens that they cut my Right Guard allotment back to once a month. And look how nappy my pelt has gotten since we can't shampoo anymore. It's disgraceful.

**Woodchuck 1:** Could be worse, buddy boy. See that guy down there on the end?

**Woodchuck** 2: Yeah. What the hell kind of varmint is that, anyway?

**Woodchuck 1:** A weasel. Willy the Weasel.

**Woodchuck 2:** That's Willy? My God! What happened to him? He's naked as a newborn skink.

**Woodchuck 1:** They tested that new eight-blade shaver on him. Hey, Willy! How you doin' down there?

**Willy**: Freezin', man. Anyone got a blanket? Someone turn up the thermostat a notch, will ya?

**Woodchuck 2:** I thought they weren't testing shavers on us anymore.

**Willy**: So did I. But the other night they grabbed me out of my cage, strapped me in a barber's chair, lathered me up and went after me with the new Gillette Habeus-Corpus-Due-Process Shaving System.

**Woodchuck 1**: Whoa. Sounds serious.

**Willy**: No kidding. The first blade stands the hair up. The second reads it its rights. The third asks for reasonable bail. The fourth denies it. The fifth files an appeal. The sixth pronounces the hair guilty beyond a reasonable doubt. The seventh reads the 23rd Psalm. And the eighth cuts it.

**Woodchuck 2**: Must have been horrible.

**Willy**: Actually, it was a nice, comfortable shave. No knicks or cuts or violations of the Miranda Grooming Rule. I think I got a fair shave. Then they doused me with Hai Karate. It's just that without my fur, I'm colder than an otter navel on an iceberg.

**Woodchuck 1**: You know, if one of us could escape, we could let the animal rights people know that they are still testing grooming products on us.

**Woodchuck 2**: Well, I'd go, but I'm scheduled for a perm next week. And God knows I could use it. I haven't been able to do a thing with my bangs since they stopped testing the Gillette White-Trash-Trailer-Park-Big-Swoop-of-Hair-in-the-Front Gel.

**Woodchuck 1**: Yeah, I guess you're right. It's not such a bad deal living here. Especially since they quit testing those Epiladys on us. What genius thought that ripping underarm hairs out with a machine was the way to go?

**Woodchuck 2**: They had one big Christmas sale and after that, the hair-yanking machine bit the dust. Thank goodness.

**Woodchuck 1**: Willy's happy it's over. He was part of the Epilady-testing program.

**Woodchuck 2**: Must have been hair raising.

**Willy**: Ha. Ha. I don't want to talk about it. My pits still haven't recovered.

**Woodchuck 2**: Sorry, Willy. Hey, someone down there turn up the thermostat! Yeah, you, the muskrat with the pompadour. Little help! We got a freezin' weasel down here!

# A Little Respect for Rusti

Rusti, the disgruntled orangutan, has been sort of the Rodney Dangerfield of animal inmates at the Honolulu Zoo, forced to live alone in a small enclosure for many years while other animals luxuriate in African savanna-type spreads. He almost had to leave Hawai'i because there wasn't enough money to build him a new home. If you wandered by his hovel, you might have heard him mumble, "I'm tellin' ya, I get no respect."

But now he's got a swanky 8,168-square-foot bachelor pad complete with bedrooms, a day room, an open sky cage and a banyan tree. The best thing is that the new digs come complete with a hot chick. That's right, Rusti's going to be shacking up with an orangutan babe.

Her name is Violet, and by orangutan standards she's a hottie: big, hairy, strong...with dreamy eyes. She's 28 years old, three years older than Rusti. Hopefully, Rusti's into older females. Actually, Rusti's been alone for so long, he'd probably be happy to hang out with a cross-dressing octogenarian panda.

I was a little worried when they brought Violet over from the San Diego Zoo, where she no doubt left a few broken hearts. Rusti wasn't in the best shape to go "a-courtin'," as Jed Clampett used to say. He was over 300 pounds (Rusti, not Jed) and who can blame him? Sitting around in his cramped quarters, with nothing to do but watch *Wild Kingdom* all day on the tube and eat bonbons.

I urged Rusti to start some cardio work and maybe try the South Beach Hairy Primate Diet. No more carbs for you, my man. You've got a babe in your midst. Violet didn't come all the way to Hawai'i to meet King Kong. You're a good-lookin' ape, Rusti, but right now your face is the size of a manhole cover.

I don't know if he listened to me. It's hard to tell with orangutans. They act like they are listening but they could just be staring at your hair, wondering, "Hmmm, are there any mites in there? I could use a snack."

The plan was to keep the two orangutans separated by a fence so they could make eyeballs at each other from afar. Eventually they'd get to "socialize." But no Rusti Juniors would result. Violet, it turns out, is a hybrid, a combination Sumatran and Bornean orangutan and so is not allowed to breed. But that doesn't mean the two kids won't be allowed to snuggle in their state-of-the-orangutan-art hacienda.

This is all good news for Rusti, who's been getting the short end of the banana for years.

He's sat in his small enclosure while celebrity apes such as Koko, the hotshot "talking gorilla," is offered 70 acres on Maui. Nobody bothered to teach Rusti sign language. If they had he might have said, "Look at this place. It's not big enough for an aardvark to change his mind. And those monkeys over there, that place is like the Taj Mahal. And what do they do? Spend the whole day throwing poo at visitors. I tell ya, it's not fair. The kinkajou's got a hot tub, I got a mud puddle. And I don't like the way that elephant is lookin' at me. Back off, big stuff, I'm not into inter-species dating. I'm tellin' ya, I get no respect."

three
——

# Welcome to Charleyworld

*"Some mornings it just doesn't seem worth it to gnaw through the leather straps."*
—Emo Philips

I was riding on a Honolulu city bus one day, sitting next to a guy who claimed to be a regular reader of my newspaper column. He asked me where I get ideas to write columns day in and day out. I told him that basically, a lot of what I write about is weird stuff that actually happens to me. I told him how I made a horse cry; how I walked through a restaurant thinking girls were "checking me out" when I actually had a stream of toilet paper trailing behind me. There were plenty other things I didn't tell him. Like how I had to sell newspapers at high noon in a chicken suit because I was dumb enough to bet that a certain team would win the Super Bowl; how I got tied up to a desk at 'Aiea High School by some punks and the teacher walked out; how my brother and I almost killed ourselves hitching a ride on the back bumper of a milk truck. He seemed unconvinced that strange things seemed to happen to me. Then the bus pulled over and a large local man lumbered from the back of the bus to exit. But first, he turned on me, only me, and began to shout threats. I never saw the guy before. He finally left the bus, threatening, "Next time, white boy. Next time." My seat partner looked at me—along with everyone else on the bus—and I said, "Welcome to Charleyworld."

# A Painful Childhood

My earliest memory involves being chased through the yard by a little neighbor girl armed with a fork. I was only four, and the girl was about the same age. I think she liked me, but I guess she had trouble expressing it. Or maybe she was just a psychopath.

The memory is just a few frames of action forever burned into my brain by the sudden yet intense surge of adrenaline. I can't even see the girl's face anymore. She didn't get me. I was a quick little cuss back then.

The incident brings to mind a couple of observations: first, the need for parental supervision of children who have access to sharp metal objects, and second, it is amazing that any of us actually survived childhood.

For me, the "Florida Fork Fiasco" was just the first of many death-defying, or at least serious-injury-defying, occurrences.

It was followed not long after by the "Morocco Death Dive From a High Slide into the Concrete Episode." We were living in Morocco, which is sort of like Disneyland for a five-year-old boy if Disneyland was 147 degrees and overrun with goats and scorpions. I don't remember exactly how the plunge happened, except one second I was at the top of a very high slide and the next second I was on the ground without having used the sliding part of the slide at all. I cleverly broke my fall with my head. I still have a small knot on my forehead 45 years after the fall. You'd think that some adult would have covered the concrete with something. Sawdust? A mattress? A bit of felt? How had I managed to fall 15 feet onto the only part of the Sahara Desert not covered with sand? Someone should have been sued, but there weren't many lawyers in North Africa at the time.

The slide plunge was nothing compared to the "Georgia Milk Truck Bumper Bummer." A milk truck would rumble through the dirt streets of our neighborhood every few days. It would stop at our house, then our neighbor's house, then a few houses down the street.

It did this every time it came. Until my brother and I decided to sneak onto the back bumper while the driver was dropping off milk. Our little butts barely had enough room on the bumper as the truck took off.

The truck started to move but amazingly did not stop at our neighbor's house. It picked up speed. It failed to stop at the next house. We were terrified. My brother said we had to jump before it reached the highway, but it was already going too fast. Crying, we pushed ourselves off the bumper and went tumbling into a ditch. Miraculously, we were not injured. Naturally, the truck stopped at the next house.

It also was in rural Georgia, too, that we played "See Who Can Stay on the Railroad Track the Longest with the Train Coming." We always jumped off before the train got closer than a few telephone poles. But the way the conductor blew the horn, you'd think we were tying someone to the tracks. We also broke the windows of the passing caboose with rocks. We were a right little Jesse James gang back then. Until a railroad detective came to our house and had a chat with Dad. You'd think that Dad would have been at least pleased that we hadn't lost a limb during our train escapades. He chose to dwell on the negative aspects of the enterprise. Who knew that railroads had detectives?

The "Arizona Bullet-Firing Adventure" was probably the most dangerous thing we survived. We were about eight by then, and our parents dragged us to a friend's house. We were bored, so we poked around the house until we discovered a box of .22-caliber bullets. With only a vague understanding of how a bullet works, we decided to try to fire off a few by hitting them with rocks in an alley. For the next few minutes we sprayed bullets all over, aiming at a garbage can but never hitting it. How we didn't shoot ourselves in our skinny little legs is a mystery.

When we got to Hawai'i, near-death experiences were common. Every time friends and I entered the ocean to surf, something bad would happen. I once saw a list of the most dangerous beaches in Hawai'i, and I figured out that I had been injured at every one of them. I've had my arms dislocated in wipeouts, I've wrenched my neck hitting shallow reefs, sea urchin spikes have stabbed into my feet and jellyfish barbs have slashed across my body. I've been dragged out in rip currents and held under by undertows. Once, while riding a wave, a friend kicked his board into my head, almost knocking me out. A jagged piece of fiberglass from his board cut my shoulder. The wound really needed stitches, but since we had cut school to go surfing, I couldn't go to the hospital.

Bullets, trains, milk trucks, girls with forks…all I can say is that it is lucky for our parents that someone didn't get really, really hurt. I mean, what kind of adults would leave a box of bullets lying around where kids can find them? And are you going to tell me that they couldn't hear the sound of gunfire? And didn't my Dad know if he let me borrow the car on a school day I would end up at the beach instead of in class? The lack of parental control when I was growing up is just shocking.

# Hold Your Horses

My horse's name was Thor, which was ironic, because that's exactly what my thighs were after riding for 45 minutes.

Thor was a big horse. A huge horse. Nevertheless, I detected a hint of fear in his eyes as I approached, as if he were thinking, "My God, that large man isn't going to get on me, is he?"

Let's be honest here. If body types were supermarkets, I'd be more of a Safeway than a 7-Eleven. OK, Costco. But when it comes to horses and fear, it's always been a one-way street: me afraid of them. It's a fear that I have nurtured through the years. So, as I approached Thor, I enjoyed the satisfaction of seeing that the hoof was on the other foot. Yeah, big boy, I'm getting on you.

We were at Kualoa Ranch for my daughter's 11th birthday. She wanted to go horseback riding. She had wanted to go when she turned 9, but I told her it was against my religion. I'm a devout coward. It took two years for me to get around to taking her. And, so there we were in the paddock and the mighty Thor was pleading with his eyes with Judy, one of our guides, not to let me get up on him. But I walked toward the little portable stairway at Thor's side. A little kid started up the steps to get on Thor, but Judy shooed him away.

"No," she said, pointing to me. "This horse is for the big, uh, the large, uh, I want that gentleman right there." You don't put a 7-Eleven-sized kid on a Costco-sized horse.

So I climbed aboard, and Thor and I lumbered out into the waiting area, something like the Titanic leaving the dock. The other riders marveled at my gigantic mount. A big man on a big horse is an impressive sight.

I felt good. I wasn't afraid of this horse. I wasn't going to embarrass my daughter. I was going horseback riding. Yeah, man, I felt good. I was in control.

Then Thor began to, well, urinate. I mean he was going to town. It was a prodigious flow. A veritable Niagara. The other riders were amazed. It was unceasing. Incessant. Unremitting. In a word, astounding. It flooded the ground. It formed a vast lake. It spread across the dusty corral like a tidal bore. Birds took flight. Babies cried. Small buildings were being washed away.

And then a little girl, standing next to a gate with her mother, pointed in my direction and said, "Look, Mommy, that fat man broke his horse."

Well, so much for dignity. I tried to make the best of the situation. "Bear up, old boy," I said, patting Thor's neck. "We'll get through this."

The waterworks stopped and Thor adopted an expression of tired resignation.

With all the other riders mounted, we began a lovely 45-minute trek along the flanks of the Ko'olau Mountain range on the Windward side of O'ahu. Thor was a champ, leading the way along a trail. Kualoa Ranch, the expansive green backdrop for many movies, like *Jurassic Park*, spread out below us. In the distance, just off shore, Chinaman's Hat, a small pointy-topped island and bird sanctuary, poked out of a still, blue sea.

It was incredibly beautiful. And, although we weren't galloping across the tundra or jumping hedgerows, we were technically horse-back riding, something I once vowed I would never do again.

On a day 37 years before, my father had taken my brothers and me out into the country in rural Georgia to go horseback riding. We rented horses that, from what I could tell, had no interest in leaving the barn. Mine walked reluctantly through a pasture, last in line. My dad yelled at me to keep up. Finally, a few hundred yards from the barn, my horse simply stopped. "Hit him with the switch," my Dad counseled. Was he crazy? Me, a little kid, was going to hit this enormous creature with a stick? I tapped him a few times, but the horse wouldn't move. My Dad gave up and told me to go on back to the barn. I slowly pulled the horse's head around. Gradually the barn came into view in the distance. I nudged the horse in the ribs gently with my heels. And then…bam! It was like the gates being thrown open at the Kentucky derby. My horse tore through the Georgia countryside like a demon possessed. I barely held on, tears stream-ing back horizontally into my ears. We covered those several hundred yards in what I believe was a Georgia State Horse Racing record. My little white hands had to be pried from the reins by the rancher. I was taken off his back like a mannequin and propped up against the barn, staring blankly into the distance. The horse munched happily on grass several yards away, acting like nothing had just happened. But something had happened. I had learned something. Never, ever again would I climb onto the back of any animal bigger than I was, and that included dogs and sheep.

But 37 years later, there I was upon the back of good old Thor. Trustworthy Thor. Thor who walked at a reasonable pace through the rolling ranchland. Thor, who very possibly could have been on animal tranquilizers, considering a Merry-Go-Round pony could have outpaced us. Or maybe Thor felt just a little overloaded.

Back at the stables, I dismounted like a true horseman, without the use of the lubbers' stairs. I'm not sure if horses can look relieved, but Thor was doing a pretty good job of it. I patted his neck one more time.

"See?" I said. "That wasn't so bad was it?"

Judy led Thor away to a holding pen crowded with other horses.

My daughter and her friend were ecstatic with their ride. It had been a great afternoon. We agreed we would have to come back again. Somewhere in the holding pen I thought I heard a horse begin to cry.

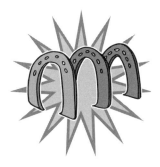

# The Institution of Marriage

I'm often stopped on the street and asked, "What is the secret to a long, happy marriage?" I always reply, "Honey, how many times have I told you not to ask that question when we're on the street? If you're going to be sarcastic, wait until we get back home."

Now, when we are at home I ask the questions. Like, if a husband hasn't "strayed" in 25 years of marriage, does that mean he's saved up at least three "seven-year itches"? (To the young readers in the crowd, a "seven-year itch" is that time in a marriage, or so I've been told, when one partner's eye may rove a bit, dragging the whole body along with it.)

"Sure," my wife said. "You've got three seven-year itches. But after all that time, there's not much worth scratching."

We are approaching our 25th wedding anniversary. The 25th anniversary is dedicated to gold, I believe. Or else tofu. Or perhaps an obscure root vegetable. I have several weeks to figure it out. I'm sure that the first three anniversaries are celebrated with rock, scissors and paper. If injuries ensue, the fourth wedding anniversary is celebrated with legal counsel.

But again, it's all hazy. After 25 years of marriage, everything's hazy...memory, waistline, distant street signs, nearby street signs, memory.... Did I say street signs? What isn't hazy is jiggly, and what isn't jiggly is brittle and what isn't brittle has obviously been replaced.

With more than half of all marriages ending in divorce, you have to wonder about the institution of marriage. As an institution it isn't exactly Alcatraz, which is to say, escape-proof. People escape from marriage all the time for reasons as silly as a possible impending homicide. To stay married for 25 years these days without perimeter guards or German Shepherds patrolling the grounds is something to celebrate. Actually, to stay married for 50 years is something to celebrate. To stay married for 25 years is something to be vaguely confused about. Twenty-five years? But that's impossible. I'm only 27 years old. Aren't I? What does that street sign ahead say?

From a husband's point of view, the secret to a long, happy marriage, or at least a long one, is to watch the movie *Fatal Attraction* at least once a year. That's the movie in which Michael Douglas has a weekend fling with Glenn Close while his wife is out of town. They have a jolly time, but then Close starts stalking him, threatening to ruin his marriage and his life. Douglas and his wife end up drowning Close in a bathtub. Or shooting her. Something in the killing line. Husbands and wives sometimes just don't do enough together these days.

Although I may joke about seven-year itches, my eyeball is as the eyeball of a Roman statue, unroving, frozen in place with only the love of my life in focus. At least I think it's the love of my life. It could be a street sign.

# Revolting Appliances

M y life is on the fritz. At least all the gadgets, gizmos and electronic appliances in my life are on the fritz. When one electronic device goes on the fritz, it's a bother. When all your electronic devices go on the fritz en masse, is it a sign of a massive right-wing, New World Order, revenge-of-gizmos conspiracy?

First the broiler unit in the oven stopped broiling. Fine. Who needs to broil? No broiler means no cheese toast, so I considered the death of the broiler the first step in my new health program.

Then the color went out on the big television set. I never heard of such a thing. Sure we have other televisions, but they are part of the television support staff: a small one in the kitchen, a weird one for downstairs, an old one for the bedroom, a tiny hand-held television for those television no-fly-zones between rooms. But this was the primary household television, the big Sony Trinitron. How could it lose color? I mean, it's a *color television.*

You can do without a broiler but you simply can't live without a 28-inch Sony. We aren't barbarians, after all.

So I muscled it carefully off the table and onto a blanket. I pulled the blanket along the floor until I got to the stairs. I gingerly levered it down one step at a time. (The term "28-inch" refers to the length of the hernia tear you'd receive if you tried to lift it by yourself.) I slipped it off the last stair onto my skateboard and rolled it out to the garage. Using the secrets of Egyptian pyramid builders, I managed to get it into the back of the pickup truck. I drove to the little television repair place. I went in and told the large, swarthy fellow behind the counter that my television had betrayed me and gone to black and white for no good reason. He told me to bring it in. I said it was too big. He said something like "Oh, jeez," walked out, picked it up as if it were nothing more than a box of Charmin toilet paper and carried it in the store. What a showoff.

A week later I got the television set back after paying the internationally mandated gizmo-repair unit price of $300. I asked the guy what he had done to fix it and he told me something deliberately complicated that he knew I wouldn't remember.

Two months later the color went out again, and when I called the TV repair shop again, everyone in the shop had taken to speaking only Esperanto. The only English phrase they knew was "Call back later," which proved remarkably effective in breaking my spirit.

Since then, the pace of the decline of modern civilization has hastened. The toilet makes strange, high-pitched noises when flushed and leaks water on the floor. I looked inside the back of the toilet and found it complex, wet and yucky. So I put a metal bowl under the drip.

The smoke alarms began to mock me with little peeping noises when my back was turned. Do they mean to tell me there is a very tiny fire somewhere on the premises? Or do these little electronic death wheezes mean that either the batteries are low or the smoke alarms have simply lost the will to live?

The toaster simply refuses to toast. It always had an attitude, but I attributed that to its being a Cuisinart toaster. Toasters with French names apparently think they are too special to actually make toast. I don't know why, but I decided to try to fix the toaster myself. I unscrewed about 500 screws and removed the metal toaster casing. The innards were just as mysterious and perplexing as I knew they'd be. Using an acetylene torch, jackhammer and a small pair of tweezers, I delicately ripped out the innards and spread them on the counter. At least the Cuisinart doesn't look so smug anymore, scattered over the counter like a downed aircraft.

One ceiling fan has commenced changing speeds at will, and the others seem listless and depressed. I was really disappointed in the ceiling fans. They always had my love, adoration and respect. Why would they turn on me now, so to speak? How bad can life be when your job is simply to spin in circles?

What will happen next? It's almost like living inside a Stephen King movie. Perhaps my electric chainsaw will turn on in the middle of the night and begin to do battle with my weed-eater or clothes dryer. Something must be done. The appliances are revolting. I'm thinking of calling in a handyman. Or at least an exorcist. While the phones still work.

# If I Had a Jackhammer

I've been taking advantage of the dry weather to do a little work around the yard. And all I can say is I hope it starts to rain real hard very soon before I kill myself.

First of all, my "yard" is a lava flow. That is, my house is perched on a hillside that apparently is an ancient tongue of lava. This makes landscaping quite an adventure. I never thought a jackhammer would be part of my yard-implement arsenal.

But as I've found out, the jackhammer is essential, especially when you accidentally come across a centipede the size of a rake. With the spade attachment on my jackhammer, I was able to quickly tock-tock-tock-tock the centipede into four equal sections faster than that guy on *Yan Can Cook* could have done with a cleaver. To my horror, the centipede sections then proceeded to flee north, east, south and west. That was when my long-handled, flat-scooper shovel came into play. I was able to splatter the scurrying arthropod units before they could escape and, I suppose, regroup. Having the right tools for the job is important to yard care.

For instance, I found out early that the standard pickax is useless on a semi-vertical yard like mine. Yes, there is something resembling dirt there. But it is only there to hide the solid lava. I found this out the first time I swung the pickax—with all my might—into what I supposed was regular old dirt, only to have it meet the lava with a quite amazing result. A tremor began at the metal end of the ax and traveled up the wooden handle where the energy was transferred into my hands. The tremor then shook through my arms and traveled throughout my entire body until I was suspended horizontally to the ground, vibrating like a 220-pound tuning fork with my teeth chattering and my eyeballs knocking around in the sockets like marbles in a whiskey tumbler. That pretty much did it for yard work that day. In fact, I don't think I stopped vibrating for a week.

That's when I began looking for a jackhammer. And I found a little electric beauty. It cost $500, but the guy at the store assured me it would pay for itself, seeing as how it costs $75 a day to rent one. And, he added, all my neighbors of the male variety would be jealous to learn that I own a jackhammer.

He was right. Owning a jackhammer puts you in a category of yard warrior that used to be reserved for guys who own their own chainsaws. Now, everyone has a chainsaw, even men who live in condos. I have a nifty little 16-inch electric chainsaw. (The size of yard implements is important, you see.) I also have a weed-eater that can cut through telephone poles. So you can imagine that when I put on my golf shoes (essential slope footwear) on a sunny Saturday and arm myself with my jackhammer, chainsaw and weed-eater, the neighbors know I mean business.

They also know there's a good chance that I'm going to hurt myself.

The problem with using heavy-duty yard machines instead of manually operated picks and shovels is the ability to do quick, serious bodily harm.

For instance, I discovered that when using even a small chain saw, it is important not to hold it in one hand and slash through branches as if you are brandishing a machete. Once I nicked the palm of my free hand with the saw, just enough to cut a shallow furrow where the lifeline had been. Luckily I wasn't hurt badly. But I realized that I had come within centimeters of having to learn how to write columns using only letters on the right side of the keyboard. (I+ migh+ look plinty phunny, mon.)

So far I haven't jackhammered any of my piggies to market or into the neighbor's yard. But the weather seems to be holding, and that's a bad sign. Like all weekend yard warriors, I'm praying for rain.

# The Chainsaw: Man's Best Friend

A friend and I were watching a home improvement show in which a man and woman who never yell at each other put in an automatic garage door in about 37 seconds. (I'd love it if just once, the lady would accidentally drop a cement block on the guy's head or he'd accidentally affix her pants to the wall with a nail gun. That would be reality TV.)

Because I had just installed an electric garage door opener at my house, I knew that the process was just a little more complicated than Ken and Barbie made out. They accomplished their task using little more than a cordless screwdriver.

"Where's the chainsaw?" I asked.

"Chainsaw?" my friend said. "You used a chainsaw to install an automatic garage door opener?"

I paused. I considered the implication of his question silently. Was he suggesting that a chainsaw is not a proper implement to use in the installation of a garage door opener? I didn't want him to think I was a novice in the home improvement game. But, yes, I had used a chainsaw in my garage door opener installation, so I stuck to my guns.

"Yeah, I used a chainsaw," I admitted.

"Why?" he asked.

I couldn't believe a guy could be so dumb.

"I used the chainsaw because I had cut the cord to my electric circular saw in half a few weeks earlier," I said. Man. Some people just don't get it.

Then I realized that on these television home improvement shows you never actually see anyone cut the cord to their electric circular saw in half. In fact, you never see them using an electric circular saw to cut down a large bush, which is what I was doing when I cut my saw's cord in half.

I was using the electric circular saw on the bush because the chain to my chainsaw was busted. The reason the chain was busted was because I had used the chainsaw on bamboo instead of using my machete, which I figured was too dull to do the job. You sometimes get into vicious circles in yard and home improvement work.

Here is something they never tell you on those home improvement television shows: when you've got an electric circular saw designed to cut lumber and you use it to cut the trunk of a fairly large bush in your yard, pay attention to where the electric cord is. The cord could be hidden in the branches, and when you cut through the cord, you can get quite an electric jolt, just before the saw goes dead. Trust me on this.

The thing is, I figured that if I had used my dull machete on the bamboo, it might have bounced off and bruised my leg. (Hint No. 2: Keep your sharp lawn implements as dull as possible so that when you screw up and hit yourself with them, they won't cut you.)

Another friend of mine cut through his calf muscle and Achilles' tendon with a really sharp machete while pruning a palm tree. This could have been avoided if he used the right tree-trimming implement: an electric jigsaw. Now, the electric jigsaw is generally used to cut shapes out of plywood. But I used mine to cut down a small banyan tree and it worked very well. It had been sitting in my tool cabinet for years because I had no plywood that needed cutting up. So when the banyan tree became a problem, I decided it was time for the jigsaw to contribute to yard maintenance. I'll have no shirkers in my tool shed.

Anyway, I eventually replaced the chain on the chainsaw, which is about as fun as putting pajamas on a badger. So when I went to install the garage door opener and found that a wood beam in the garage was just a little too low and needed to be cut, the trusty chainsaw was ready for service.

These television shows are fun to watch but they seem to have nothing to do with the reality of home improvement. For instance, you never see Ken and Barbie using a jackhammer. Even when installing a garbage disposal.

# Stumped at the Dump

One day, the garbage-to-energy HPower plant is going to blow up, and it will be my fault. That's what a large, agitated man at the garbage transfer station on the Windward side of the island was telling me as we stared thoughtfully at an equally large and agitated tree stump sitting in the back of my pickup truck.

This gentleman, in a dirty white T-shirt that didn't quite cover everything that needed to be covered in the stomach department, was one of the dump guys who categorize your debris by some incomprehensible system (Animal, vegetable, mineral? Green, brown or fuchsia? Pre-Colombian vs. Late Eisenhower? Combustible or not?) before telling you where on the property to dispose of it.

The tree stump under consideration managed to get by the gatekeeper at the entrance to the dump. Of course, it was camouflaged by other refuse, including a small refrigerator suffering from a fatal case of bad attitude. The fate of the refrigerator was incontestable. It was bound for the sad little community of discarded appliances behind the transfer station building, where castoff refrigerators, stoves and washers stand like Stonehenge, were it sponsored by Sears.

But the tree stump, that was the stumper, so to speak. I always like to let a professional do his job, so I stood by while my man considered the gnarled root mass the size of an engine block. The problem seemed to be that 1) the dude at the gate shouldn't have let it in to begin with, and 2) now that it was at the transfer building, just where should it go? Anything flammable goes into the large pit where it is hauled to the HPower plant and burned to make electricity. In my case, electricity to power the chain saw I use to cut down trees in my yard and haul to the dump. It seems a pretty good symbiotic relationship.

The tree stump in question was probably burnable, but, man, it was big. It might get jammed in the garbage ingester at HPower, causing a fiery explosion of accusations as to exactly which idiot let this root bomb into the system. That's when my guy pointed out in a friendly way that one day HPower was going to blow up, and it would be the fault of people like me who sneak around trying to feed enormous tree portions into a facility designed for milk cartons and paper towel rolls.

I nodded my head in a meaningful way as if to say I appreciated his counsel. But the fact was either the stump stopped here or it accidentally fell out of the truck somewhere down the road. I definitely wasn't taking the brute back home with me. Trying to be helpful, I suggested that we ignore the fact that it was a tree stump and pretend it was, say, a couch. "Where would you dump an old couch?" I asked.

Ah! It was the breakthrough we needed, and soon the stump was in the large Dumpster reserved for broken furniture, smashed televisions and, from what I could see, lost dreams. As I drove home I reflected that those pitiful things would be buried in a landfill to slowly but gradually remain there for all time. But my tree trunk, saved from the fiery pits of HPower, perhaps one day would push a fragile green sprout through the landfill crust and live again.

# Calls of the Wild

"Mrs. Martha Heimlichmaneuver in?" the caller asked.

"Heimlichmaneuver?" I replied.

"Hemmingshtimer?" he tried again.

"Keep going," I urged, "you're getting warm. Here's a hint: it starts with 'M.'"

"Memmingshturger?" he ventured.

"Oh, you're soooo close. Go, boy, go."

"MemminGer?" he asked.

"Fabulous! Now, lose the hard 'g.'"

"Memminger!" he said triumphantly.

"Now, ask the question all together from the top," I directed.

"Is Mrs. Martha MEMMINGER in?" he asked, like someone one who just won the lottery.

"No," I said.

"All right," he said. "Please tell her I'll call her back later."

"What's this about?" I asked. "This is her husband, Mr. Heimlichmaneuver."

"I'm from Flaky Financial Services, and we'd like to offer Mrs. Memminger a credit card with (reading) rates-so-low-that-we-practically-have-to-pay-her-for-using-it."

"Let me guess," I said. "You aren't the CEO of this operation, are you?"

"No," he conceded

"You don't even work for the company, do you?"

"Ah, not exactly," he said.

"In fact, you are just some boiler-room telephone weenie who gets paid to cold-call names off a list, am I right?"

"Sounds kind of harsh when you put it that way," he said.

"I've got a question. I get about two of these calls a day now. And, all of the callers ask for my wife. Why is that?"

"We're not allowed to speak to the husband," he said.

"Allowed? By whom? The Cold-Calling Financial Shyster Network Police?"

"Look, man, they give me a list of names and I dial the numbers. I'm sorry if I've bothered you. I've got to go."

"No," I said. "You called. I just want a little information. You seem like a financially astute individual. You are, aren't you?"

"Well, I own my own Yugo," he said.

"A titan of industry!" I erupted. "Now, tell me, Mr. Gates, do you ever do business with someone over the phone?"

"Does Pizza Hut count?" he asked.

"Not unless you are buying a franchise."

"Well then, no, I guess not," he said, sadly.

"So, when it comes to *your* money, would you do business with a complete stranger who calls you up while you are just sitting down to dinner and can't even pronounce your name?"

"Hell, no!" he said happily, as if he had just aced a high school personal hygiene exam.

"So, why would you expect me to have anything to do with Flaky Financial Services?"

"Geez, mister, why do you think I asked to talk to your wife?" he said.

"Yeah, I know. Wives are easily dazzled by a suave and sophisticated financial charmer like yourself."

"You'd be surprised," he said, proudly.

"Actually, I wouldn't. That's what makes the whole thing so depressing, that these kind of insulting, brain-dead tactics actually work."

"It's a crazy world," he said philosophically.

"Well, listen, I figure by keeping you on the line, I've saved at least 10 other innocent victims from having their dinner interrupted by you. It's been a pleasure."

"Don't mention it," he said. "And you'll tell Mrs. Heimlichmaneuver that I called?"

"Oh, yeah."

# Child Labor Day

As you sip your beer or lemonade, munch your barbecue and nap under the shade of a beach umbrella, today—Labor Day—is a good day to consider how we are wasting one of the country's greatest assets: our children.

How much longer can we ignore the fact we are squandering this great resource? I conducted an informal poll and was shocked to learn that hardly any children have jobs. It's true. Go up to any kid and ask how many jobs he's holding down and you'll find out that he's not even working part-time. Millions of children could be just sitting around on their butts, expecting adults to do all the work.

Child labor used to be the backbone of industry in this country. You could say, child labor *made* this country what it is. *(Editor's note: History isn't this writer's strong suit, so any historical references from here on out should be taken with skepticism.)*

In fact, it was all those children working 100 years ago that allowed the adult labor unions to pull a fast one on Congress and get it to set aside one day a year to "celebrate the working man" with a phony-baloney day off. I think it was Matthew Maguire, a machinist, who came up with the idea of Labor Day in 1882. He was standing around tinkering with one of his machines and it suddenly hit him, "Hey, this industrial revolution is a drag. I'm pooped. Let's take tomorrow off."

And they did. But the kids kept working, so nobody really missed the adults. Maguire later tried to get Labor Week legislation passed and even floated the idea of setting aside 1884 as "Labor Year" when no one would work at all, but President Grover Cleveland smacked him around and told him to quit loafing. *(Editor's note: Grover Cleveland was not even president until 1885.)*

But those were the golden days of child labor. Everywhere you looked, industrious children scampered around, their faces charmingly blackened with coal soot or their little fingers toughened by picking cotton. *(Editor's note: Machines were being used to pick cotton by then.)*

*(Columnist's note to editor: Quit butting in. And besides, who do you think were* driving *those cotton-picking machines? Children.)*

Anyway, somewhere along the line, a bunch of do-gooders decided that children shouldn't have to work because they were too young. Can you believe it? And the children played their part perfectly. They smeared on extra coal soot on their faces and didn't comb their hair so that they would look like poor little rapscallions. *(Editor's note: "rapscallion" means scoundrel or rogue. The word he was reaching for is "ragamuffin" or perhaps "tatterdemalion," which would refer to something pitiful, much like this column.)*

Before long, the law prevented children from working. And these little slackers have been getting a free ride ever since.

As we relax and take a much-needed rest on this Labor Day, we should consider the benefits of striking down anti-child-labor laws and putting this vast segment of our economy back to work again. Sure, they might not have enough education yet to operate computers, and they're too short to drive buses, but there are lots of tasks children can do. They can dig ditches and build rock walls. They can work in the fields and stitch baseballs. Working will give them pride and make them strong.

If you think the economy's good now, just think how great it will be when several million children join the labor pool. As Thomas Jefferson said, "If you want your children to keep their feet on the ground, put some responsibility on their shoulders."

*(Editor's note: It was Dear Abby who said that.)*

# Blood from a Couch Potato

I'm a pint low. I've never been a pint low before. At least, not on purpose and not since I was a kid, when spilling blood was a fairly regular occurrence.

This time I'm a pint low on purpose, and I'm waiting to see what effect it has. So far, none. Taking a pint of blood from someone my size is kind of like taking the vermouth out of a martini.

It took months of prodding but my wife finally forced me down to the Hawai'i Blood Bank to surrender a pint of my precious bodily fluid. She's an old arm at giving blood. She gives by the gallons. Blood runs in her family. Or at least *from* her family. Her dad has filled more barrels than OPEC.

Giving blood is a good thing. It's a needed thing. And it's something that I've wanted to do for a long time. The fact that I didn't give blood until I began closing in on my 43rd birthday tells you something about my desire to give blood vs. the reality of giving. It took a while to psychologically prepare myself.

The main thing was I had to separate the act of giving blood from the act of bleeding. I hate bleeding and always have. It's one of the things I hate worse than just about anything else. Except pain. Pain and bleeding, those are the biggies. In my mind, giving blood was simply bleeding profusely into a plastic bag.

But I got by that. Mainly because I started to feel guilty. I'm a big guy. I've got lotsa blood. Why am I hogging it? Especially since it takes 200 donors a day to meet Hawai'i's blood needs.

That doesn't sound like much. Two hundred. But you gotta figure, a person can only give blood every eight weeks. That means there needs to be at least 11,200 *different* people giving blood over that eight-week period. Now, *that's* a lot.

And so, faced with the shame of being married to a woman who is a veritable fountain of blood donorship and the fact that more than a few of my friends and family have needed blood over the years, I went down at lunch the other day to be tapped.

It turns out it's not a big deal, really. You fill out some forms. They want to make sure you aren't carrying any infectious diseases, like HIV or hepatitis. They poke your finger with a sharp gizmo that doesn't hurt as much as it surprises. They take a few drops of blood to make sure you have enough iron.

Then they lead you to the comfy reclining chairs and hook you up like a stereo. It's really anti-climactic. It doesn't hurt. If you don't watch what's going on, you'll think the guy is just taking your pulse or something. The pint bag fills in about 5 to 8 minutes, depending on, I don't know, how much blood you've been hoarding. Since I haven't given blood for 42 years, mine simply shot out and I filled the bag before I could get through the first few pages of *Newsweek* magazine.

Then they unhitch you, plug the puka with a piece of gauze and a bandage, and that's it.

I know, I'm sounding like one of those guys from *Invasion of the Body Snatchers*. "It's OK. It doesn't hurt. You'll be fine. You'll be one of us."

But it's true. It doesn't hurt. You will be fine. And you will be one of us. See? Now I'm one of them. I'm a blood giver. I don't have to feel guilty now around the holidays when I hear those pleas by the Hawai'i Blood Bank for more donors. It's a sad but accurate fact that more blood is needed during the holidays than just about any other time.

So, all you people under 110 pounds, you're off the hook. You're a little too light to give blood. But the rest of you wusses, the people who have never given blood before, call the Hawai'i Blood Bank and make an appointment. You'll miss one lunch, but you might save a couple of lives.

If I can do it, you can. It's all right to be a pint low during the holidays. In fact, it's the best present you can give.

# The Naked Truth

A ll I want for Christmas is my two front teeth and one of those new Playboy dolls. Those two items may not seem to have anything in common, but trust me, as soon as I get around to telling my wife I want the limited-edition, 16-inch replica of Swedish blond bombshell Victoria Silvstedt for Christmas, my two front teeth will be in immediate jeopardy.

Maybe I won't mention the Playboy doll to my wife. Maybe I'll order it, wrap it, address it to myself and hide it under the tree. On Christmas morning, I'll act surprised and say, "Look what Santa brought me! An anatomically correct replica of the 1997 Playmate of the Year! I must have been a *good boy*!"

Yeah, like she's going to buy that. What the hell was Hugh Hefner thinking when he decided to issue this new line of collectable Playmate dolls?

Obviously, the target market is degenerate old married men. But how are we supposed to obtain the blasted dolls if it means becoming the victims of spousal homicide?

Dolls have always been bad news for me. I remember when the first G.I. Joe action figures came out. I couldn't wait. I went down to the toy store every day to see if they had arrived. I told my dad how they came with guns and helmets and boots and were just like the little plastic Army men except you could move their arms and legs.

Finally they came in, and I pulled my Dad to the store. He looked at the G.I. Joes and said, "Hey, those are dolls. You're not getting a doll. What are you going to want next, a tiara and pink tutu?"

Those might not have been his exact words, but they capture the spirit of the moment. I never did get a G.I. Joe. Or a tiara, although I wondered for years what the hell a tiara was.

When my daughter was born, we moved into a new world of dolls. She had a ton of Barbies, and all of them were naked. It apparently was too much trouble to put the little costumes back on the dolls once they were taken off. At one time there were four naked

Barbies sitting in a little red Barbie convertible sports car in the middle of her room. Those Barbies had a better life than I did.

Sarah's favorite doll was a "My Size" Barbie, a doll of frightening height, maybe three feet tall. That doll, too, ended up naked. But as Sarah got older, she lost interest in dolls and was actually embarrassed to have them around when cousins came over. I'll never forget the time she stuffed the naked "My Size" Barbie under my wife's and my bed without telling us. How could I forget? It was about that time a workman came to install a mirror in our room, which entailed moving the bed. The workman shoved the bed aside, and there was the naked, nearly life-size doll.

"It's my daughter's," I sputtered. His eyes said, "Yeah. Right."

Despite my track record, the limited-edition Playboy dolls still seem pretty cool. And they are going to be worth a lot of money one day, just like the first-edition G.I. Joes. I'm sure my wife will understand that the only reason I want a Playboy doll is as a long-term investment. I'll tell her that if my Dad had let me get G.I. Joe when it first came out, it would be worth about $50,000 today. She'll see the wisdom of getting several first-edition Playboy dolls just to supplement our investment portfolio. Yeah. Right.

# The Piano Purchase

Someone should publish ground rules for garage sales. We recently bought a piano at a garage sale, and frankly, it was a messy affair.

We had been looking for a used piano for ages. Prices seemed to range from $1.37 to $43,000. I don't know much about pianos. I know they are chiefly made up of a bunch of white keys with a gaggle of little black keys sprinkled haphazardly over the keyboard. When you poke at one of the keys, the piano emits a sound. This is called "music."

There are all kinds of pianos, but they all share one basic characteristic: They are extremely heavy and hard to move. There are upright pianos, not-so-upright pianos, pianos with shadowy pasts, grand pianos, baby grand pianos, fetus grand pianos and pianos with only visions of grandeur.

When you don't want a piano, several thousand of them will be for sale at dirt-cheap prices. When you actually want one, they are suddenly scarce. And the harder you look, the more expensive they become.

If you find a reasonably priced piano in the paper and call the number listed, you are met with derisive laughter, seeing as how the piano was sold 12 minutes after the newspaper hit the streets. Knowing this, when my wife and I saw a piano for sale in a recent newspaper for $500, we raced to the garage sale address so we could be first in line. It turned out we knew the people selling the piano. The wife was happy to see us. She introduced us to her husband, who was talking to another couple on hand also interested in the piano. We entered the house, letting the other (older) couple go first out of courtesy.

As we looked at the piano, the older couple asked some serious piano-related questions. I quickly scanned the instrument. Yes, it seemed to have the requisite splatter of white and black keys.

"We'll take it!" I announced, favoring a pre-emptive strike. The other couple blanched. They claimed they had the right of first offer because they had entered the house first. This was the closest we had come to having a shot at buying a piano, and I wasn't going to lose it on a vague technicality. Yes, I said, they had entered the house first because the threshold was not wide enough for all of us, and we were just being polite to our elders.

They insisted that garage sale etiquette held "first come, first served," and since they were first in the house, they had the right to make the first offer. I refused to budge. It was a standoff. The old dude looked pretty spry, but I figured I'd win if he had to wrestle for it. Instead, I suggested we flip a coin, which I thought was sweet of me. The piano owners—awkwardly caught in the middle of an escalating garage sale battle that theoretically could lead to bloodshed—quickly agreed that would be fair. The other couple grudgingly went along.

I flipped the coin, and the grumpy old codgers (forget courtesy, this was war!) called it. They lost. In the driveway, feeling magnanimous, I apologized to the couple for the way things worked out. The wife was crying. The husband hissed, "You're only making it worse!" They climbed in their Mercedes and drove away.

I don't think we were wrong in how we handled the situation, but someone ought to put together some firm rules for garage sales. If that couple had been a few decades younger, I might have been in real trouble.

# TheSpitter

I'm not a bus rider. I love the concept. I support mass transit. But being cooped up with lots of people makes me feel weird.

But the other day I had to walk downtown. And because the Kona winds have made Honolulu hotter than one of Kathie Lee's sweatshops in Nicaragua, I thought I'd pay a buck and ride TheBus back to the News Building in cool comfort. TheBus, that's what they call it. For some reason, someone in marketing thought it would be clever to run the "The" and the "Bus" together, in sort of an alphabetic collision passing as art. It says "TheBus" on the sides of all the buses in Honolulu just in case you can't figure out what that enormous rectangular vehicle rumbling down the street is. I didn't care. I wasn't so much interested in TheBus as in TheAirConditioning.

I know there is some logical method to the routing and numbering of buses. And I know that with just a little effort, even I could figure the system out. But it seems like lottery number chop suey to me. So I told my wife my plan to walk downtown and take the bus back. After she stopped laughing, she told me exactly which buses I could and couldn't catch. I could catch any bus with a number in the 50s and would be deposited right on the News Building's doorstep. I could even take selected 40s. But I definitely didn't want to take any ones, twos or threes; they went around the island, or something. She seemed to recall that 20s were bad, too. My eyes began to glaze over.

"Stick to the 50s. Take any bus with a 50 number and you'll be OK," she said.

Secretly, we both knew it was hopeless.

I moseyed downtown to do my business and then stood at a bus stop near Nu'uanu Avenue. Waiting is not something I'm good at. I'm into instant gratification. If I have to stand around in one place, out in the open, I feel vulnerable. But if I was going to escape the heat, I'd have to stand my ground waiting for TheBus.

A little old man came up and stood beside me. He looked like a gentleman in his dapper suit, but he suddenly cleared his nasal cavity with a loud inward snort and then ejected the offensive missile in the general direction of my Reeboks. I looked at him like he was insane. He looked at me like I was insane. A few seconds later he let another salvo fly in the other direction. I guess it was his idea of courtesy.

I looked at him again trying to register my revulsion at his continued expectoration. He looked at me as if to say, "What? It wasn't even near you."

Not knowing bus stop etiquette, I didn't know if I should verbally reprimand him for his behavior. Other people had gathered at the bus stop, and they just ignored him. So I did the same. Several buses stopped. They were all of the wrong number. People got on these buses and left. Everybody except for me and "TheSpitter."

"TheSpitter" then took out a crusty-looking comb and proceeded to rake it across his head. Then he dragged his thumbnail over the teeth of the comb, shooting flecks of white junk toward the street. Then he began to dig his pinky finger into his right ear. He jammed it in there up to the second knuckle and excavated a large chunk of wax or extraneous brain matter. This, too, he flicked out into the street.

That was it. I couldn't take any more. I started to walk down King Street, thinking I could at least wait at a bus stop without such extracurricular grooming.

I reached the next stop, and no buses of any caliber were in view, so I kept walking. By the time I reached the Post Office, I was sweating like Richard Nixon, and the only buses going by were the "Dreaded Twos" and the "Hateful Ones." Even a Number 20 went by to mock me on its merry way toward Diamond Head. Had I stepped onto one of those, I would have been whisked off to mystery spots, possibly never to return without having to call my wife to pick me up. I don't think either of us could bear the humiliation of that.

"Where are the 50s?" I thought, like a man in the desert hurting for water. "Is that a Number 55 coming or a mirage?"

It was a tour bus.

I started walking again, knowing I'd be taking no bus rides that day. And just as I got back to the News Building, TheBus, Number 55, pulled up and stopped. I mopped my sweaty brow and thought bad thoughts about mass transit. And then I saw him, sitting by a window, looking very cool and dapper in the air conditioning, "TheSpitter," all dressed up and with, apparently, many places to go.

# A Bug in Your Ear

I knew the term "to put a bug in one's ear" means to get someone thinking about something, but I never truly appreciated what an exquisite focusing mechanism having a bug in your ear can be.

Unfortunately, your entire focus is on the bug in your ear, which I discovered the other day while helping my wife on the computer. I was just standing there, giving some sage computer advice, when I heard a high-pitched buzzing and then felt something hit my ear canal.

"Hey, a bug just flew in my ear," I said.

"Which one?"

"I don't know; seen one bug, seen 'em all."

"No, which ear?"

"The left one. And it's still in there."

She didn't believe me. But I started getting excited.

"I'm telling you," I said, "a bug flew in my ear. I felt it burrow inside. It's still in there."

"Can you feel it?" she asked.

"No, but I know he's in there."

God, I thought. What are you supposed to do when a bug flies in your ear? I was focusing like a madman.

"Try a Q-tip," she suggested.

"Are you crazy? That would just squish him up in there or jam him in even deeper. I'd have to wait for him to decay."

I began to realize how serious the matter was. A foreign flying object was inside my head. I didn't know what it was. It could be harmless, or it could be something dangerous, like a Brazilian Brain-Boring Beetle. What was I supposed to do? Was he sitting in there licking at the sticky insides of my ear canal? Was he already gnawing on my brain's protective membrane? Or was he just shivering in there, scared after accidentally flying into a human head cave?

It's times like these when you realize how poor your knowledge of the human body is. I tried to remember what the inner ear looked like. I knew that somewhere in there was a hammer, an anvil, a stirrup and, I believe, a candelabra. Maybe they would block the bug from going in deeper. Was there a clear path to the brainstem?

My daughter came over and asked me to help her with her homework.

"Give me an eight-word sentence using the word 'Inuit,'" she said.

Aha. Hearing damage already. "Inuit? What the heck's an Inuit?"

"Someone who lives in the Arctic," she said.

I imagined the bug chomping on the delicate nerves inside the ear

"Honey," I said, "I can't help you now. I've got a bug in my ear."

"Which one?"

"The left one."

"No," she said, "which bug? A roach? A termite? An ant?"

I shooed her away. Maybe I should pour peroxide in there.

"We don't have any," my wife said.

Maybe some beer would do it. Beer in the ear. The alcohol would kill it, maybe float it out.

"Quit worrying about it," she said. "It will probably come out on its own, if there's one in there at all."

Ha. Big words from someone without a bug in her ear.

I took the dog out to do his business. Standing on the porch, I felt a tingling by the ear opening. I sprinted back in.

"He's coming out! I feel it!"

I tipped my head sideways and my wife probed gently with a Q-tip.

"There it is," she said. "I see it. Hold on. There."

The bug lay on the counter top. It was tiny, a mere speck, nothing more than a comma with wings. Something along the gnat line.

"It felt a lot bigger when it was in there," I said, a bit too defensively.

She rolled her eyes and went back to work. I bet Inuits get more respect than this, I thought. Exactly eight words

# The Body Politic

It's that time of year when we hear all about the state of the union, state of the state, state of the city and the state of just about everything else.

And so, as has become a tradition in my household, I arose the other morning to give my annual State of My Body Address. My body used to eagerly look forward to this address. Now, there is a lot of murmuring and grousing from the various body departments as the gavel slams down and the teleprompter in the bathroom begins running. It went something like this:

"My fellow body parts, it gives me great pleasure once again to be your mouthpiece."

(Low rumble of acknowledgment.)

"The Department of Brain and I have worked hard throughout the year to represent your interests to the various doctors, pharmacists and other health industry representatives to assure that each of you is able to perform at your highest level. Our goal is to walk with dignity over that bridge to the next century. It's not necessary to run over that bridge, especially at our age. But by the same token, we don't want to hobble, limp or crawl over that bridge. In recognition of that goal, we'd like to go over some of the developments of the past year and provide a vision for the future.

"First of all, we know that some of you feel we are not getting the benefit of all the new exercise equipment on the market. Research by the Department of Brain has shown that these machines have little long-term effect on the body. So we will not be getting an Ab Roller. The fact is, we already have Abs of Steel. They are just hidden by the Tummy of Tofu. Which is just around the corner from the Buns of Blubber. This is not a criticism. It's just recognition of a few problem areas. So, buns, don't start blubbering.

"It was a very good year for some of you. Specifically, the Departments of Knees, Ankles, Toes, Elbows, Wrists, Fingernails and Ears provided laudable service during the past year. The Department of Calves needs to work on that middle-of-the-night cramping problem, and the Department of Teeth needs to try to hang on to those fillings a bit longer.

"The Division of Internal Organs seems to be functioning efficiently. The Department of Brain realizes that when it approves the ingestion of certain liquid substances the Division of Internal Organs suffers. But you do a good job of notifying the Department of Brain of your discomfort. So much so that on a few days, the Department of Brain decided to keep the entire body horizontal for a 35-hour period. Spleen, kidneys, lungs and heart were consistently outstanding. We ask that you stop hazing your fellow organs. Specifically, do not refer to your fellow organ as the 'Liver of Lava Rock.'

"As usual, we will brief you on the fine work done by the Department of Sexual Function during executive session, because these are personnel matters involving the right of privacy. But we feel the Department of Sexual Function deserves some public recognition of its outstanding performance. And so, we'll just say, 'Way to go, fellas.'

"The Office of Hair also had a particularly good year. It not only held its own on top of the head, but also began new colonies in the ears, nose and parts of the back.

"And so, overall, we'd say the State of the Body is good. There is room for some improvement, certainly. But we are ambulatory. The Committees on Chemical Analysis report cholesterol and other serum levels within safe operational parameters. And our external surfaces are generally free of obscurities.

"As we approach the end of this millennium, we encourage you to continue strive to be the best body parts you can be. Remember, ask not what your body can do for you, but what you can do for your body. Thank you. Have a nice day. And now, hit the showers."

(Wild applause.)

# A Hairy Situation

You know you're getting old when your hair starts turning against you.

One day your hair is your friend, the next day it is on the move. It grays, it migrates, it disappears altogether. After you pass 40, your hair has things to do, its own agenda.

Hair that has been perfectly happy perched on top of your head decides to go south for the winter of your lifetime. That's why you see guys who are completely bald on top and yet whose backs look like horsehair throw rugs. And it doesn't stop there. After a few years it leaves the back and heads for the, well, you know, the posterior area. Your bottom. Maybe it's nature's way of providing the elderly with natural pillows to protect brittle bones. (Which brings up a completely unrelated question: why are bottoms called bottoms? To be correct, the feet should be called bottoms. They are at the bottom. The bottom really should be called the middle.)

Doctors used to think that when people went bald, the hair on their head simply disappeared. It doesn't. It just reassigns itself, sometimes to the most alarming places. I always feel bad when I see an otherwise dignified-looking older gent with tufts of hair springing out of his ears, for instance.

I grew a mustache when I was about 18 to make me look older. At least, that's why I thought I grew it. I had not shaved it off for decades. Then it turned on me, started getting prematurely gray. I know, all gray hair is premature, but this was really uncalled for.

I am not old, damn it, and I will not have my mustache making people think I am. So I shaved it off. In a minute the mustache was gone, after nearly 30 years of faithful duty in the middle of my face.

I shrieked when I looked in the mirror. I realized then why I had grown it in the first place: I have no upper lip. Nothing. There's the nose, then the little unnamed thingy under the nose and then... teeth. I was a Wes Craven nightmare: The Man with No Lip. What had I done?

My daughter had never seen me without a mustache. I was sure that if she saw that the old man had neither a mustache nor an upper lip, it would be too much for her. She might never recover from the shock.

But what could I do?

I tried little patches of silver duct tape, but I looked like a robot version of Hitler. I thought of applying black Magic Marker, à la Groucho Marx. But it was no good. I was stuck. The lipless wonder, staring into the mirror while shards of my grayish former mustache mocked me from the washbasin.

My daughter apparently wasn't traumatized by my missing mustache. But hysterical laughter also was not a comfort. I'm not an overly sensitive person, but I think hooting and pointing at someone's face is impolite.

Luckily, mustache hair is hardy. The mustache grew back quickly, and it went to work providing not only facial balance, but also, thankfully, camouflage.

The mustache-shaving incident has had some unfortunate long-term side effects. When my daughter needs to be scolded, I can no longer say, "Don't you give me any of your lip, young lady."

Well, I can. But then she says, "Why not? You can use all you can get."

# four

## There's Something About Maui

*"There is wild whale sex going on in the water around Maui."*
—Dave Barry

Research claimed that the air route from Honolulu to Maui was one of the busiest in the country. It didn't say that the route from Maui to Honolulu was similarly busy, so I guess there must be about 90 million people living there now. It doesn't seem that way, through. Maui is an oasis within an oasis. Some people come to Hawai'i from the mainland to relax. And then some of those go to Maui to *really* relax. And, then, as Dave Barry points out, a lot of whales swim from Alaska to Maui every year just to have sex.

Celebrities love Maui. Beatle George Harrison bought a beachfront place but discovered that a public right-of-way to the beach edged his property. He became a prime tourist attraction, just behind Mt. Haleakalā. I've written often about plans to give "Koko the Talking Gorilla" 70 acres on Maui. In a state like Hawai'i where most of us measure our property in feet and inches, giving a gorilla—even one who can use American Sign Language—70 acres of the most expensive real estate in the world seems a bit excessive. Doesn't Georgia need talking gorillas? Then I found out that Oprah had bought a bunch of luxury waterfront property on Maui. And I thought, how perfect is that? You have the Queen of Talk Shows possibly being neighbors with a talking gorilla. They've got to get together for a TV special. (Koko (signing): "I love what you've done with the lānai, Oprah, but where do you keep the bananas?" Oprah: "Koko, the fabric in your tree house is so *toile de jouy*.")

When it comes to neighbor islands, Kaua'i has the lush rural landscapes, the Big Island has the volcanoes, O'ahu has the people and Maui, well, Maui is that beautiful movie star who looks great right out of the shower in a funky bathrobe. And when she's dolled up...fuhgeddaboutit. But here's a few things you probably didn't know about Maui, and they don't involve whale sex....

# Missionaries Gone Wild

W hen most people think of Maui, they think of that play-ground of the rich and famous. If Hawai'i is the "bou-tique state" of America, Maui is the "boutique island" of Hawai'i. (To digress even further, Wailea is the "boutique region" of Maui, the Grand Wailea Hotel is the "boutique hotel" of Wailea, the Tradewinds Boutique shop is the "boutique boutique" of the Grand Wailea Hotel, and the ritzy hat-and-sandals corner of the Tradewinds Boutique is the "boutique of the boutique boutique." We could keep going, but I believe we would eventually enter the realm of "boutique molecules," which are still largely theoretical.)

Anyway, Maui is a hot, fashionable place. It was dubbed "Maui Nō Ka 'Oi," or "Maui Is Best," by a completely neutral yet far-sighted public relations guy working for the Maui Convention and Tourist Bureau in, I believe, 1936. There were only four tourists on the island at that time, and the PR guy was holding them at gunpoint to keep them from boarding a boat to the Big Island, screaming "Maui nō ka 'oi! Maui nō ka 'oi!"

Things have changed. There are thousands of visitors to Maui today, and the only way to get them to leave the island is at gunpoint. Some residents tired of traffic and high prices have suggested chang-ing Maui's motto to "Maui—*No Mo' Nō Ka 'Oi.*"

But few visitors realize that behind Maui's glitz is a rich history of, well, history. I particularly like the 19th-century history because up to that time, things were pretty boring. It took six million years for the island to even pop above sea level, and then a lot didn't hap-pen for many, many years after that. Legend has it that Maui was named after the demigod Maui, so it was lucky there. It would have been weird if Maui had been named after the demigod New Jersey. (A "demigod" is part-man/part-god, which is different from a Demi Moore, which is part-babe/part-goddess.) The demigod Maui was known as the "trickster." One of his tricks was to lasso the sun with a rope made of coconut fiber, and if you don't think that's tricky, try it some time. He was going to kill the sun for moving across the sky too fast but spared his life. So the sun was lucky there.

Polynesians settled on Maui (the island, not the demigod) a way long time ago, and everything was cool except when pitched, bloody battles were fought between the indigenous residents. (Where's the demigod when you need him?) But life was pretty sweet until "Western contact" in the 18th century. In 1778, Captain Cook sailed by and saw 10,000-foot Mt. Haleakalā and wasn't impressed. He had just come from the Aleutian Islands and Alaska, where mountains were mountains. He noted "some kind of a hill" on Maui and continued on. A year later he was killed on the Big Island. Too bad he never heard of the whole "Maui Nō Ka 'Oi" thing.

But it was in the 19th century when things started happening on Maui. In 1819 the first whaling ships arrived. They were the *Equator* from Nantucket, the *Balaena* from New Bedford and, I believe, the *Surf and Turf* from Atlantic City. The first missionaries showed up in 1823, so the whalers had four relatively fun years. The missionaries did everything they could to bring themselves and Maui residents closer to God, mainly by buying up a lot of land and getting rich.

But the whalers and sailors held their own, and in the early 1940s a traveling minister named Henry Cheever described Lahaina as a hellhole and "a sight to make a missionary weep." We can only imagine that any sight that would make a missionary weep would make a sailorman jump up in the air and click his heels together.

Herman Melville, who would become one of America's premiere pain-in-the-butts for high school literature students everywhere, arrived in Maui on a whaling ship in 1843. About that same time, Kamehameha III reportedly left Maui for Honolulu because, you know, when Melville shows up some place, there goes the neighborhood. (Melville later referred to Kamehameha III as a "fat, lazy blockhead and a drunk." I suspect he was not on the same island as Kamehameha III at the time.)

Melville was fashioning his notes on sailing and whaling into books at the time, books that later would become *Moby Dick* and *Billy Budd* but whose working titles were *Moby Bernard* and *William Buttoutski*.

Whaling was Maui's major industry for many years, mainly because whales returned every November to Maui to give birth and were easy to catch. In 1844, 326 whaling ships stopped in Lahaina, causing Hawai'i's first aquatic traffic jam. Lahaina was a very happening place, full of drunks and prostitutes and missionaries and drunken missionaries. It was like Spring Break in Panama City, Florida, is today. It was then in Lahaina that the first "Whale Burger in Paradise" restaurant opened and a naughty little pamphlet made the rounds called "Missionaries Gone Wild."

There were nearly 4,000 people living on Maui then. A census showed that of all the houses, 59 were made of rock or wood, 155 were made of adobe and 882 were made of grass. There were relatively few wolves going around blowing down houses back then, so the people living in grass houses were lucky there.

But by the late 1850s the whaling industry collapsed, mainly due to a conspicuous lack of whales. Where did they go? You killed them all you fat, lazy blockheads, said Kamehameha III. Ha, ha, ha. It wasn't just that the most of the whales had been killed, but that the world was turning to the use of coal for lighting and heat, and coal was much easier to spear with a harpoon. (Nevertheless, Melville's attempt at a sequel to *Moby Dick*, entitled *Moby Charcoal Briquette*, never found a publisher.)

Ironically, the economy of Maui was saved by the California Gold Rush of 1849, which brought business from over-eager miners who overshot California. (What are we doing here? Where's the gold?)

The next big thing to happen on Maui in the 19th century was a visit by Mark Twain in 1866. He said nothing but good things about Hawaiian royalty, being a little swifter on the social niceties than Melville. He climbed Haleakalā and spent hours pushing large boulders into the crater until someone told him to knock it off.

So that's pretty much the history of Maui in the 19th century. Things have changed so much. Pushing boulders into Haleakalā Crater is now a federal offense. But riding a rental bicycle down the flank of the volcano at Mach-4 isn't. If Captain Cook sailed by Maui now, he might notice all the sophisticated telescopes at the top of Haleakalā. Or he might just note, "some kind of a hill with stuff on it." I tell you, between Cook and Melville, I'm surprised any visitors are allowed on Maui at all. So the rich and famous shopping in the Tradewinds Boutique are pretty lucky there.

(Many thanks to the book *Insight Guides—Hawai'i* for background for this piece.)

# Send in the Dogs

Maui public schools are considering bringing drug-sniffing dogs on campus, which eventually could lead to the use of drug dogs at all public schools. That could lead to an increase in the number of dogs going to schools to learn how to sniff out drugs in order to meet the huge demand for drug-sniffing dogs. And of course, that would lead to an increase in the number of drug-sniffing dogs who search drug-sniffing dog schools for drug-using dogs.

One of the ugly secrets of the entire drug-sniffing-dog industry is that 38% of all dogs who undergo drug-sniffing-dog training succumb to the temptation to use drugs themselves. These poor creatures can be seen covertly trying to sniff the white lines off parking spaces and trying to light crack pipes behind the drug-sniffing-dog school gym, an enterprise that is exceedingly difficult without thumbs.

Dogs drummed out of the drug-sniffing-dog schools are shuffled into other programs, such as bomb-sniffing-dog schools, where they either get their drug problem under control or end up as part of the wallpaper.

Drug-sniffing dogs used to be the coolest law-enforcement canines on the block. But as terrorism became a serious problem, the bomb-sniffing dogs became the top dogs, sort of like Vin Diesel versus Chevy Chase. Drug dogs are increasingly relegated to public intermediate and high school campuses where, on a big day, they might uncover an alcohol lamp in a science lab or half a can of Bud Light in the teachers' lounge.

Bomb dogs get the high-profile gigs at airports, train stations and youth hostels in any city hosting International Monetary Fund global economy conferences.

I attended public school in Hawaiʻi, and we didn't need drug-sniffing dogs. That's mainly because everyone pretty much knew who the drug users were. You'd just stick your head in any art class and, well, there they were. I signed up for an art class when I first enrolled in public school here because I was lazy and thought it would be an easy A. It turned out to be a dumping ground for some of the most incorrigible druggies and misfits in the school. Apparently anyone seriously interested in art took French.

I don't know if having drug-sniffing dogs on Maui public school campuses is a good thing or not. A lot of schools now have a "zero-tolerance" policy on drugs, which means that when a drug-sniffing dog rats out a kid to the authorities, that kid is tossed out of school. This has several effects. First, it makes the drug-sniffing dog feel pretty good. Then it allegedly makes the schools safer for other students. And finally, it allows the expelled student to immediately pursue his career as a criminal, where he'll no doubt eventually end up in a prison patrolled by drug-sniffing dogs.

# Maui's Big Cat

Authorities have been searching Maui forests for months, looking for an animal believed to be a leopard or jaguar or mountain lion or something along the more frightening "large cat" line, but have turned up neither hide nor hair of the creature. Nor whisker nor toenail, for that matter.

In fact, after being hunted by some of the most imminent wildlife officials that could be scared up both locally and regionally, the fearsome feline appears to be largely hypothetical. Sure, residents have reported large catlike animals knocking over their garbage cans and scaring the bejesus out of their smaller pets, but there has not been a real sighting of the presumed predator yet. Which raises the question: if there is a big cat out in the wild and it's so hard to find, then it's obviously not bothering anybody, so why not leave it alone?

It reminds me of the time someone said they thought they saw a crocodile in Nuʻuanu Reservoir near the Pali, a reservoir that nobody even swam in or anything. But people couldn't rest until the existence of the animal was confirmed, which it finally was when somebody shot the poor thing off a log while it was napping. It turned out it wasn't even a crocodile, it was a caiman, a smallish crocodile-like animal, a croc lite, if you will. It was not a danger to anything other than frogs, and small ones at that. And the slaughter of the snoozing reptile achieved nothing other than to prompt copy desk editors to come up with painfully cute headlines such as "Caiman Went."

With the rumors of a mysterious large cat in residence, Maui is quickly going from being called the Valley Isle to the Weird Animal Isle. First it was to be home to Koko the "talking" gorilla. Then we learned it is overrun with formerly domesticated parrots that fly around in large squadrons, bombing the landscape with weed seeds in their droppings. Now a potentially dangerous cat is roaming around.

A distinguished "big cat" expert, appropriately named Bill Van Pelt (a colleague of the equally renowned duck expert Percival Van Coot) hoofed it around the wilds of Maui and reported that there probably is a large cat out there. How can he be sure? He found several enormous hair balls and a cat toy the size of a bicycle hidden in some brush. Just kidding. He saw pictures of a small deer that had been killed that showed "classic big cat characteristics," which I suppose means the cat played with it for a while before leaving it on some neighbor's doorstep as a gift.

Van Pelt thinks the cat is living on tree rats, which causes me again to ask why don't we leave it the hell alone. Let it eat tree rats and, if we can teach it to catch those crazy bombardier parrots, let him eat those, too. In my book, any cat that kills large, tree-dwelling rats is considered a "good kitty."

Although Van Pelt returned to the mainland without seeing the cat, he did organize the installation of automatic cameras that might snap a picture of the animal as it passes by at night. (If they get a picture of a large cat flashing a "shaka" sign at the camera, they'll know they have something.) The expert also advised that if you come across the big cat, back up slowly. Do NOT turn and run. Yeah, right. If I even hear of someone seeing the thing, I'm going to run like hell. And I don't even live on Maui.

# When George Lived on Maui

Y ou have to feel sorry for former Beatle George Harrison. All he wants is to be happy, as the song says. He just wants to enjoy his personal chunk of prime 'āina on Maui, but people keep tromping all over it. Specifically, his neighbors are using an easement through Harrison's 63-acre lot to get to the ocean, and some of them, gasp, have had the audacity to point out Harrison's hacienda to friends as they walked by.

It's not like tourist buses are staging a "Magical Mystery Tour" in his driveway, but you have to understand, privacy and security are important to former Beatles. After all, John Lennon was gunned down practically on his own doorstep, and Harrison was attacked by a guy with a knife last year at his London home.

Harrison's still pretty young, and, frankly, he'd like to sing "When I'm 64" when he's 64, and he rightly feels he might not get there if people keep jabbing metal objects into chest.

The Hawai'i Supreme Court is involved in the case, which means he might be 64 before the case is ever settled. He must be feeling a little bitter having to go though this legal hassle at this point in his life. After all, Koko the Gorilla, who can talk in sign language, is to be given 70 acres on Maui, and she won't have a bunch of baboons tromping across her land.

Right about now, Harrison is probably thinking about rewriting some of those classic old Beatles songs to reflect what he's going through:

**"All Things Must Pass":** Sunrise doesn't last all morning/ A cloud burst doesn't last all day/But the idiotic neighbors/Just won't ever go away....

**"A Hard Day's Night":** It's been a hard day's night/Calling lawyers and filing suit/It's been a hard day's night/The judges were stuck with a big galoot....

**"Help":** Help! I need some fences/Help! Not just any fences/ You know I need da kine, ohhhhhh, electric's fine....

**"This Boy"**: This boy, spent a whole lotta dough/That boy, didn't tell me, though/That there was a big stinkin' easement/ Running through the property he stuck me with, that weasel....

**"I Want to Hold Your Hand"**: Oh, yeah, I'll tell you something, I think you'll understand/When I slap that subpoena, right in your slimy hand, I want you off my land!/I want you off my laahaahaahaand/I want you off my land!....

**"I Feel Fine"**: Judge was good to me, you know/Said my land was mine, you know/ I won on appeal and I feel fine....

**"Hey Jude"**: Hey, Judge, don't be afraid/Tell those plaintiffs, to go and take a hike/Remember, they've gotten under my skin, so you can begin, to make it right....

**"The Ballad of John and Yoko (Ballad of George and Koko)"**: Standing in a forest in Maui, that monkey'll have it better than me/They'll keep tourists away, so that Koko can play, and the day trippers will swarm over me.... Christ, you know it ain't easy, land, that chimp don't deserve/Forget the gorilla, how about a Beatle Preserve?....

**"Yesterday"**: Yesterday, all my troubles seemed so far away/ Now they're just o'er there, thataways/Sunburned haoles wearing plastic leis/I hope they'll fall from those rock cliffs one day....

**"All You Need is Love"**: There's just one thing that can be done/To keep these gawkers off your lawn/There's just one thing that'll get them gone/All you need is love (and couple of vicious dogs)/ All you need is love (and a team of lawyers)/All you need is love (and some pepper spray)....

# Maui's Nude Beaches

I n olden days a glimpse of stocking was looked on as something shocking, except at Maui's Little Beach, where, heaven knows, everything goes. At least everything did go, including shirts, shorts, bikini tops, bikini bottoms, inhibitions, propriety and, depending on who exactly was getting naked, the view.

State officials are going through their scheduled 10-year hot flashes and angst attacks as they once again discover that—shock!— people are tromping around butt-naked on a beach in South Maui.

This affront to the dignity of the state takes place at Mākena State Park at a beach called Little Beach, which is right next to a bigger beach called Big Beach. (Hey, where are the lyrical Hawaiian names when you need them?) Little Beach is a secret nude beach known only to the entire naked world via the Naked People Network, which keeps track of places where people can take their clothes off in public and not get arrested. Little Beach is famous among secret, unknown naked beaches, having been rated one of the Top 10 naked unknown beaches in the world by the International Association of Clothesless Sunbathers (also known as Bare Buns without Borders).

Everyone on Maui knows that people go naked at Little Beach. But being a laid-back island, it takes about 10 years for everyone to get upset all at once about it. So now we are in the decadial (my word) state review of the appropriateness of a state-sponsored nude beach. Since nude beaches are illegal, state officials can't officially condone one; they only can allow it to exist with a wink and a nod. Or, depending on who's naked on the beach at the time, a wink, a nod, some hearty applause and requests for phone numbers.

But that's the problem with naked beaches and naked everywhere elses: people who like to take their clothes off in public are usually the last people you want to see naked. Nude Rule No. 1: ugly people get naked for free. If you want to see an attractive person naked, you've got to pay for it, or at least buy dinner.

Another fact is that the only reason men get naked on a naked beach is to see naked women. If a guy could sit fully clothed in a beach chair with a beer in his hand and gawk at naked women, he would. But then he'd be called a perverted creep. (Or so I've heard.) But if he takes his clothes off, he can gawk all he wants. Unfortunately, that's when Rule No. 1 kicks in.

five
———
# The Write Stuff

*"There are just three rules for writing, but nobody knows what they are."*
—Somerset Maugham

And I sure don't. I have written probably a few thousand newspaper columns and, say what you will about talent, that's still a lot of typing. The difference between writing columns and writing a book is that you sit down, write a book and then you're done. But you keep writing columns year after year, and then if you ever see everything you wrote in one place you have a retroactive literary hernia. I love writing about Hawai'i and life in general, but every once in a while I write for the sake of writing. Playing with words and sentences, trying to create something that will amuse, or at least interest, people who like to read. I think the key to writing columns is to have a long short-term memory, so you can get your work done quickly, and to have a short long-term memory, so you don't overly dwell on your successes or failures. And of course, ignore the rules.

# From Defective to Fective

I was reading a book recently in which one of the characters was "decapitated" (just a little light summer reading), and it occurred to me that in order for one to be decapitated, one must first be "capitated." And yet, you never see this perfectly good root used, as in, "He was a finely capitated young soldier until he called Napoleon a girly-man."

I suppose we don't employ the word "capitate" to describe people because if they are living beings, we assume they have a good head on their shoulders, or at least a workable one. Likewise, we don't use the opposite of decapitate—"recapitate"—mainly because medical science has not made strides enough for that operation to be success-ful. In the distant future, I predict there will be as many recapitated people as there are people today with new livers (reliverated people?).

But the whole decapitation thing got me thinking of what a debacle the English language is when it should be a bacle. I'm assum-ing that if "debacle" means "a big mess," than "bacle" must mean everything is just fine. ("The meeting was a bacle, everyone working quietly and well together.")

Why, in literature, are people often debased, defiled and debauched but seldom based, filed or bauched? I live in a constant state of bauch and am proud of it.

Why is an electrical gadget often defective but never fective? I have many fective appliances in my house, but they seldom get credit for it.

People often deplane or detrain but never plane or train. Instead they get "on" a train or "on" a plane, when clearly it would be safer if they went inside the things.

We deduce, declare and decline but never duce, clare or cline. Why? I'm sure that when Sherlock Holmes wasn't deducing some-thing, he was just generally ducing. And if you don't decline some-thing, aren't you, by definition, clining it?

Why do you accuse someone of deceiving you yet never give

them credit when they ceive?

You hear about armies being deployed or even redeployed, but you don't hear about when they simply ployed, or sitting around waiting to go somewhere.

Often things that are "de'd" become "re'd," but not all the time.

Declassified papers become reclassified, and when we are dehydrated we can be rehydrated. But why do we refer to it as "detox" when someone undergoes drug treatment but not "retox" when he falls off the wagon? And why are buildings demolished but not remolished when they are rebuilt? Terrorists demolished the Twin Towers, and we are still talking about how to remolish them.

Do you have to be pressed before you become depressed and praved before you become depraved? And for all the deprived children in the world, aren't there many more who are gleefully prived?

I hate to denounce our native tongue, but I think it has been nounced long enough. I'm defiant about this issue today, where yesterday I was still demurely fiant. And before I was demure, I was merely mure, a state of modesty so unassuming I decline to discuss it further.

What I cline to discuss is the decay of our language. The de-word "decay" must stop. It must be cayed or even recayed. This I solemnly declare, or at least demurely clare.

# Clothed Cap Chuns

I was watching CNN news on one of the televisions perched above a row of torture devices disguised as exercise machines at my local gym when I noticed something weird. And it wasn't the lady on the treadmill next to me, although the fact that she was talking on a cell phone during her entire workout was pretty weird.

Because of the noise created by the various mechanical pain inducers, the only way to follow what's happening on the overhead television sets is to read the closed captioning. (It's kind of interesting that the closed captions are not only there for the hearing-impaired, but also for the fitness-impaired.)

While reading the captions, I learned that a man who fled to England after allegedly killing his wife and child in America is facing "extra decision." Extra decision? Did they mean, like, an extra decision on whether to return to the United States? Then I realized that what the announcer had said was the guy was facing "extradition," which made a lot more sense.

So I started paying more attention to what the closed captions read versus what was actually being said on TV, and realized that the hearing-impaired were experiencing a different TV world than the hearing.

Now, I have been known to make up a few things in this space from time to time, but I swear that everything reported now actually happened. It started with the stock market report on Fox where, according to the captions, "blew chips" were down. How appropriate. I'm sure if I owned blue chip stocks and they were down, that would blow.

Then on another news station was a report that First Lady Laura Bush had a meeting with the pope or, according to the captioning, the "Holy Sea." I suspect the announcer had actually referred to the pope as the "Holy See," but captioning gave the comment added depth. Both the Holy See and the Holy Sea are deep subjects.

Another news program reported that in restarting its nuclear program, the country of Iraq was engaged, according to captioning, in "sable rattling." I'm sure if there were any sables to be rattled, it would be Russia doing it, where sables are thick on the ground. Iraq likely simply engages in "goat rattling," or maybe sabers, if they could find some.

Speaking of getting rattled, CNN reported that with Congressional elections coming up, Republicans were "squared to death." Squared to death? Is that because President Bush had put them in a box? The closed caption writers also had trouble with FOX's election coverage, calling them "Correctional elections," instead of Congressional. Or maybe that happened on purpose. Congress often is seen as a Federal Correctional Institution.

When I got home, I switched on ESPN where, according to the captions, announcers were discussing the "warm upstage" portion of the Tour de France. The warm-up stage apparently will be in England, which hopefully will be warm enough for the bikers.

Things also were warming up on the *700 Club*, where, according to the captions, Pat Robertson was worried about greenhouse gases causing "global warm being." I had no time to ponder whether that "warm being" was God, because Pat was now complaining that loggers were being put out of work by the "potted owl." I knew that protection of the spotted owl in the Northwest was causing loggers fits, but didn't know that drunken owls were, also. I think PETA should immediately turn its attention to potted owls. We can't have them flying around the forest in that condition.

On the *Tyra Banks Show*, a photographer was talking about bringing out "motion" in her subjects. If you can't bring out emotion, I guess motion will do.

On a daytime reality show, a woman at a cash register announced she had just "made two sails," but I could not see the nautical items to which the caption referred. Another woman hugged her friends and announced, "you are my angles," which seemed sincere yet puzzling. I guess when it comes to friends and angels, you have to know all the angles.

On C-SPAN, a retired Marine colonel claimed to be a "con duet to the troops," which would seem unfortunate. One con would be bad enough. He also said he wanted the troops "warring better body armor." If you are going to be warring, wearing better body armor is best.

I ventured over to a broadcast of a Honolulu City Council committee meeting, where various "stud eyes" were being discussed. A witness asked for a "curse sorry advisory opinion," according to the captions. I'm sure he would rather have had a cursory advisory opinion to the studies under discussion.

I don't know who or what computer program is in charge of typing out these closed captions, but my curse sorry advisory opinion is that the hearing-impaired (and victims of gymnasium torture machines) deserve better translations.

# Crimping My Style

Something occurred to my left pinky finger overnight. I think I slept on it; somehow kept it pinned under my not-so-svelte body, twisted it out of the socket, or something. This morning it felt like someone turned it with pliers 27 times. I'm not the fittest person in the world, but how incredibly pitiful do you need to be to suffer serious injury while sleeping?

If some of these sentences seem weird it's the result of my left pinky being locked in buttressing composed of wooden chopsticks enveloped in yellowish sticky strips of the stuff commonly used to secure bundles for post office delivery. The effect being—considering touch-typing is my forte—I must write this entire column without using the first letter of the 26 letters used to write words in English.

My left pinky likewise is commonly employed to strike the hindmost letter of the previously cited list of 26, not to mention the weird letter which looks like "O" but isn't. Writers get by nicely without using the "O-like" letter, which for some unknown motive insists on being used only in conjunction with the letter "u." No other letter enjoys such pointless coupling.

The 26th letter likewise is unneeded unless the writer is discussing the striped, four-legged horse-like life forms found upon the continent directly to the right of ours or one of those flying hydrogen-filled dirigibles like the one which exploded in 1937, provoking the gent reporting the notorious incident by wireless technology to cry in newbornish mode.

Writers don't need the insistent curlicue letter or the one sword fighters used to inscribe on trees with their offensive implement—but let me tell you, the other one, the first letter in line which my crippled pinky will not strike...*he's* necessitous.

Why? For one thing, without the letter which comes directly before "B" in the list of letters I'm getting tired of mentioning, writers resort to using words like "necessitous." I've gone through 23 of those periods of time during which our world circles the sun without using the word "necessitous." Until now. It induces me to cry in some new-bornish style or method (see: comportment).

The first letter is instilled with much import. He is the boss of Letter Town, the shogun, the chief. Few words get written without this guy's input. I would've been better off spending the night reclining upon some other digit. I could effortlessly write without the use of either index finger. "J," "U" plus "M" sit on the sidelines through most writing. The right pinky isn't overworked either, being brought into the proceedings simply to cough up the innocuous "P" or the periodic semi-colon.

But writing pros work through the hurt. Wrenched pinky or not, we got through this entire column without using the curiously co-dependent "O-like" specimen, the insidious sword-swipe icon or the overly industrious vowel who is forever first in line. Oh my.

# Your Charleyscope

Sometimes I think that, as a newspaper columnist, I have the greatest job in the world. Then I find out someone has it better than me. Like the people who put together horoscopes. What a great scam that is! Just make up stuff about the future and everyone buys it? Fantastic!

So I decided to try my hand at the horoscope game. I figure my predictions will be just as accurate as any of those alleged readers of the stars. So here it is: the First Absolutely True Scientific Charleyscope:

**ARIES** (March 21-April 19)—You're in a lot of danger. Ursa Minor and Cassiopeia have been fooling around behind Orion's back. If Orion finds out, he's going to be royally ticked. He'll probably cold-cock Ursa Minor with the Little Dipper. Then Ursa Major will put out a hit on Orion, and, well, this will be very bad for you, Aries. You'll be consumed by homicidal/suicidal tendencies. Best advice, stay in bed and cover your head with a blankie.

**TAURUS** (April 20-May 20)—Stay away from any Aries. Period. If you live with an Aries, get the hell out of the house quick. This is no bull.

**GEMINI** (May 21-June 20)—Don't tell any Tauruses or Aries, but I just made all that up. Actually, the Moon is in the seventh House and Jupiter's aligned with Mars. And peace will guide the planets and love will fill the sun. No, wait a second, that's that stupid song by the Fifth Dimension. So much for being in tune with the planets, huh? How come members of the Fifth Dimension couldn't use astrology to see their careers going down the cosmic toilet? Buy bonds.

**CANCER** (June 21-July 22)—Uh-oh. I see an indictment in your future. I see a drug agent planting dope under your bed. I see an FBI SWAT team outside your house. No. Don't look. Stay away from the windows! Don't stand next to any Aries in the cellblock.

**LEO** (July 23-Aug. 22)—You're losers. The whole bunch of you. Get out of my sight. I can't stand the sight of you. On the other hand, travel is indicated.

**VIRGO** (Aug. 23-Sept. 22)—Have you ever noticed the constellation Andromeda looks a little like Andre Agassi hitting a tennis ball? Either that or Errol Flynn in a sword fight with Cygnus, saying, "En garde, you filthy escargot, I shall run you through!" Just a thought. A loved one needs to be hugged. Or smacked. You figure it out.

**LIBRA** (Sept. 23-Oct. 22)—Change your underwear. The stars demand it.

**SCORPIO** (Oct. 23-Nov. 21)—No, don't change your underwear with a Libra. I meant for Libras to change underwear with each other. God, you Scorpios are stupid. Travel is indicated.

**SAGITTARIUS** (Nov. 22-Dec. 21)—Man, you are sexy. All you Sagittarius babes. I'm not kidding. Cowabunga. You light up my galaxy. You Sagittarius guys, travel is indicated, so beat it. Leave me alone with my little cosmo-cuties.

**CAPRICORN** (Dec. 22-Jan. 19)—Here's a prediction: If you are a Capricorn, everyone's going to forget your birthdays. Big surprise. Thanks, Father Christmas. I'm a Capricorn. If anyone forgets my birthday, I'm sending an Aries to their house with a meat cleaver.

**AQUARIUS** (Jan. 20-Feb. 18)—You will be extremely wet and filled with fish. Or maybe that's Aquarium. Anyway, you're in for something very bad involving water. I'd carry an umbrella if I were you. And a snorkel.

**PISCES** (Feb. 19-March 20)—World peace is in your hands. The stars indicate that only you can lead the planet into a new era of love and prosperity. You are the new messiah. No wait. Wrong chart. You will come down with a low-grade fever. Travel is indicated.

# You Too Can Write a Column!

I'm often asked how hard is it to write a newspaper column. Well, I say, in my most annoying know-it-all fashion, "It's the first two or three hundred columns that are hard. After that it's a breeze." Ho ho—what a card. But it's sort of true. I've got more than 2,000 columns under my belt (no fat jokes), and say what you will, if that's not writing, at least that's a lot of typing.

But I understand the universal urge people have to embarrass themselves in print. So, today, I will help you write your first column. And in doing so, not only will you feel the pride that comes from boring people on a massive scale; you will also be saving me from having to come up with yet another damn column.

All you have to do is circle words from the multiple-choice offerings below to create your own personal column. When you are finished, fame and fortune will knock at your door, or at least hurry past trying not to be noticed.

**Have you ever noticed that those**—a. *members* b. *knuckleheads* c. *un-indicted co-conspirators*—**over at the**—a. *City Council* b. *Legislature* c. *Ke'eaumoku Street strip club* d. *all of the above*—**spend**—a. *our money* b. *their money* c. *counterfeit money*—**hand over**—a. *fist* b. *ankle* c. *nostril*—**simply to**—a. *buy votes* b. *get drunk* c. *have sex* d. *all of the above?*

**It is**—a. *clear* b. *annoying* c. *soooooo typical*—**that our elected**—a. *representatives* b. *bozos* c. *nitwits*—**don't care about anyone but**—a. *themselves* b. *the Dalai Lama* c. *Secretary of Health and Human Services Tommy Thompson* d. *enter name of peculiar family relative here:* _____. **They**—a. *throw* b. *catapult* c. *smack*—**our**—a. *money* b. *puppies* c. *linguini*—**around like there's no**—a. *tomorrow* b. *yesterday* c. *Santa Claus*—**while we**—a. *bust* b. *break* c. *fold, spindle or mutilate*—**our**—a. *buns* b. *carbuncles* c. *children*—**just trying to make**—a. *ends* b. *cousins* c. *the Palestinians and Israelis*—a. *meet* b. *mud-wrestle* c. *converge at the event horizon of a black hole.* **How much**—a. *more* b. *less* c. *whoopee*—**are we expected**

to—**a.** *take* **b.** *make* **c.** *forsake?*

As a registered—**a.** *voter* **b.** *sex offender* **c.** *Democrat* **d.** *all of the above*—I think we should—**a.** *organize* **b.** *instigate* **c.** *turn a blind eye to*—a—**a.** *massive* **b.** *tiny* **c.** *very messy*—**a.** *recall* **b.** *bloody coup* **c.** *great big ol' topless street party*—to let those—**a.** *officials* **b.** *hopeless geezers* **c.** *future inmates*—know that we mean—**a.** *business* **b.** *to consult a lawyer* **c.** *to take a short nap soon.*

They need to—**a.** *know* **b.** *be afraid* **c.** *acknowledge bitterly*—that we are as—**a.** *mad* **b.** *giddy* **c.** *slightly amorous*—as—**a.** *hell* **b.** *Hades* **c.** *the eternal fiery abyss* **d.** *June Jones after his contract was made public*—and we aren't going to—**a.** *take* **b.** *fake* **c.** *Shake 'N' Bake*—it anymore!

I urge all of you—**a.** *readers* **b.** *pathetic losers* **c.** *naked people*—to—**a.** *phone* **b.** *write* **c.** *chastise* **d.** *stone*—your—**a.** *congressman* **b.** *psychic* **c.** *significant other*—immediately.

We should all be—**a.** *proud* **b.** *slightly embarrassed* **c.** *confused* **d.** *indifferent*—to be—**a.** *Americans* **b.** *bipeds* **c.** *perpendicular* **d.** *naked!*

There. You've written your first newspaper column. How does it feel? *Enter emotion here:* _____. I'm glad I could make your—**a.** *dreams* **b.** *nightmares* **c.** *vague yearnings for greatness*—come true.

six
—

# Aloha, Friends

*"I don't want to achieve immortality through my work,
I want to achieve it through not dying."*
—Woody Allen

Writers leave a great deal of literary chaff behind when they die, most of it pretty bad. Luckily, a few writers do leave behind a legacy of work that continues to provoke laughter, anger, sorrow, thought and enjoyment for generations after they have shuffled off this mortal coil. For me, writers like Douglas Adams, creator of the four-book "trilogy" *Hitch Hiker's Guide to the Galaxy*; gonzo journalist Hunter S. Thompson; and Patrick O' Brian, author of the 21-book Aubrey/Maturin sailing novels, were inspirations. I never met Doug Adams but got so much enjoyment and inspiration out of his writing that I was moved to write a little "aloha" column when he died. I was lucky enough to get to meet and talk with O'Brian and Dr. Thompson, whose writing also caused me to work harder at my trade. Here are a few pieces I wrote about my favorite writers, including long-time *Honolulu Star-Bulletin* "three-dot" columnist Dave Donnelly, after they failed to achieve immortality in the way Woody Allen hopes to do. Included here also is a piece I wrote after the September 11 terrorist attacks, which ran first in the *Star-Bulletin* and then was the only Hawai'i entry in *Chicken Soup for the Soul of America*, a book compiled in memory of the terror victims.

## DAVE DONNELLY
# Living Three Dots at a Time

If everyone whose name ever appeared in a **Dave Donnelly** column in the *Honolulu Star-Bulletin* showed up for his funeral service, the island would likely flip over like a rowboat ... That's because everyone from **Tom Selleck** to **the Pope** to **an Unknown Auntie from Kalihi Who Beat the Slots in Vegas** appeared in his column at one time or another ... Pity the celebrity like **Brad Pitt** or **Russell Crowe** or **the Wacky Blonde on** *Friends* **Whose Name Escapes Me** who tried to sneak into a quiet dinner at **Keo's** or **Nick's Fishmarket** ... Couldn't do it ... Someone would alert **Dave Donnelly** that they were there, what they were wearing and what they ate ... Or if a little love was brewing, like the time **Pee Wee Herman** and **Paulie Shore** were nabbed in a quiet little booth at **Kelly's Drive In** making cooing noises to each other ... Just kidding about that last item ... I made it up ... I don't think **Dave Donnelly** ever made up an item ... Didn't have to ... Had spies all over the place ... Waiters, busboys, PR types, flacks, sycophants, politicians, all kinds of people feeding him stuff to fill more than 30 years of columns ... **Dave Donnelly** wrote what is known in the newspaper world as a "three-dot" column ... That's because items generally were set off by three dots ... like those back there and these right here ...

Legendary San Francisco columnist **Herb Caen** put three-dotting on the map ... He and **Dave Donnelly**, who spent most of his vacations in San Fran, were buddies ... When they got together, someone was going to get drunk ... both someones ...

**Dave Donnelly** held court for many years at the legendary **Columbia Inn,** next door to the News Building, where he had his own reserved stool at the "Round Table," and **God** help the clueless wretch who accidentally sat in it ... **Lisa Kudrow** ... She never sat in **Dave Donnelly's** seat ... I just remembered she's the one who plays the **Wacky Blonde on** *Friends* ...

All kinds of famous people used to come bow down to the beer mug of **Dave Donnelly** at the Round Table over the decades

... People like **William** *"Jake and the Fat Man"* **Conrad** and **Jack Lord** and **the Pope** ... Although I'm not sure about **the Pope**, but I wouldn't be surprised ...

Eventually the venerable landmark **Columbia Inn** was torn down in favor of a car dealership, and **Dave Donnelly** gave up adult beverages and ... well ... it was the end of an era. But **Dave Donnelly** found a new stool to sit on and kept dishing out the dots and putting people's names in **boldface** ... Keeping a record of their lives, really ... An incredible archive of life in Hawai'i ... I know the high points of my life are documented within those dots ... And I feel honored ...

**Matt Damon, Tom Cruise, David Letterman** ... Don't really have anything to say about those guys ... It's just that I was getting a little mushy in the previous item ... And wanted to get more famous names in here ... like **Cher** ...

All I know is that **Dave Donnelly** ... who passed away last week ... made Hawai'i a better place ... Aloha, **Dave** ...

## ERNIE PYLE
# Patron Saint of Beer-Drinking Columnists

P UNCHBOWL CEMETERY (April 18, 1995)—I wasn't really ready for the strong emotional reaction I had when I finally found the grave of Ernie Pyle. It's not like I'm not familiar with the National Cemetery of the Pacific. My Dad, a decorated Vietnam veteran, is buried here in Punchbowl crater. I'm familiar with the nondescript little gravestones that lie flat along the ground to make the mowing easier. They all look alike. And there are thousands of them. Because this was just a day after Easter, the crater is filled with flowers: anthuriums, torch ginger, orchids and Easter lilies.

Even though I had never been to Ernie's grave, I figured I could find it without asking for directions. My guess was that it would be by the main pavilion area, near that huge statue of Columbia, which most people recognize from years of watching the opening sequence of the television show *Hawaii Five-0.*

So I began walking in that direction, reading headstones as I walked. The death dates were in the '70s and '80s, so I knew I had a way to go. Strangely enough, I was here because today is National Columnists Day. And it is no coincidence that National Columnists Day falls on the anniversary of the death of Ernie Pyle. Ernie is a kind of patron saint of columnists.

Ernie is our spiritual leader because he was a cool little guy. Author Samuel Eliot Morison called him "a frail little man, a gentle soul who hated war, who had come out to the Pacific…to tell the American people…how the ordinary soldier and sailor felt."

An Associated Press writer described him as a disheveled 42-year-old balding hypochondriac who was a delightful drunk.

The soldiers he wrote about remember him as a brave little bastard who hung out where the action was and told stories of their lives with an elegant simplicity that hasn't been matched since.

So you can see why columnists nationwide picked Ernie as our guy. As columnists go, they don't get any cooler.

It was 50 years ago today that Ernie should have ducked. While riding in a jeep with some soldiers on some flyspeck of a Pacific island, he was picked off by a machine gun.

I figured that it would be easy to find his grave. I thought his grave would be piled with flowers. I wandered around the area carefully avoiding the Easter eggs, lei and flowers scattered among the headstones. I knew I was getting warm when most of the dates of death became 1945.

Finally I found it, sandwiched between two gravestones on which were simply etched "Unknown." There was no pile of flowers on Ernie's grave. Just two vases with some wilted orchids and a rain-sodden lei.

I don't want to get mushy, but finding little Ernie here, just about a driver and a nine-iron from my Dad's grave, was, well, pretty intense. Ernie would have gone to Vietnam and, man, what columns he would have written. Ernie would have gone.

I brushed some of the dried grass from Ernie's headstone and placed a fresh lei of orchids and a cold can of Budweiser. I was going to wish him a Happy Columnists Day, but that sounded kind of weird. So I just said, "Cheers."

## HUNTER S. THOMPSON
# My Gonzo Lunch with the Doctor

KĀNEOHE, Hawai'i (Feb. 23, 2005)—Hunter S. Thompson
and I didn't hit it off when we met in 2002 at the Kahala
Mandarin Oriental Hotel. In fact, I apparently grated on
his nerves something fierce, because, when not sipping from among
the half-dozen beverages laid out before him, he repeatedly pleaded,
"You've got to settle down" and, I seem to recall, "Shut up." In other
words, it was what I gathered was a fairly normal sit-down with
the legendary gonzo journalist and semi-professional dabbler in
pharmacopeia.

I was happy to sit quietly and sip my beer (I declined the
human growth hormone nasal spritzer being passed around the table)
and listen to him reflect on life and politics. He was here to once
again cover the Honolulu Marathon for ESPN online. We didn't talk
about the marathon at all because, you know, who cares? I was just
happy to be hanging out with Hunter, as any writer of my genera-
tion would have been. My only regret is that after the lunch I wrote a
rather snotty newspaper column about the meeting, having fallen into
that trap of trying to be as cool as the guy you are writing about. One
of Hunter's friends was furious with me. He thought I had been disre-
spectful of him. That I had hurt Hunter's feelings. You would think
that it is hard to hurt the feelings of a writer who has created a public
persona as a hard-drinking, drug-taking outlaw who's called U.S.
presidents "swine"—and called just about everybody else "swine," too,
for that matter.

But I regret that column now, even though Thompson apparently was not bothered by it, mainly because, I learned later, he never
read the thing.

*Fear and Loathing in Las Vegas* was required reading for aspir-
ing writers in college, and pity the poor professors who had to slog
through our pitiful attempts to mimic Thompson's style. I secretly
believed that his propensity to ingest a mind-numbing menu of pills,
potions and draughts was merely myth, a way to shock a bunch of

Cuban Missile Crisis, post-Vietnam, Cold War babies who weren't easy to shock. But then again, I had one college professor who made smoking marijuana a compulsory part of the curriculum, so who knows. Maybe Thompson's life was a trunk-load of pot, coke, speed, LSD and God knows what else. He sure looked the part when I met him. Forget drugs—I was surprised that he could drink gin, scotch, champagne and coffee all at the same time, which he was doing during our lunch.

But to focus on his carefully manufactured public profile of excess is to miss the point that he was a hell of a writer. Every sentence was fun to read. And he was politically incorrect before anyone knew what that was.

Before I left that liquid lunch with Thompson, I gave him a yellowed copy of *Painted Veils*, the infamous 1920 book by James Huneker that critic H.L. Mencken called "an absolute riot of obscenity." Coming out as it did at the time of the Comstock book-banning laws, Huneker's book had to be published as a private edition. Huneker was the Hunter Thompson of his day, exposing hypocrisy and the dark underbelly of the ruling classes.

Something happened when I handed Thompson that little paperback reprint, which originally had sold for just 35 cents. He seemed genuinely moved. Although we didn't "hit it off," I felt we had shared just a moment when he knew that I knew that behind his boozy veil he was up to serious writing business. Then he put another cigarette in his holder and lit it, told me to settle down and took a sip of one of the several glasses in front of him.

I thought of that moment when I heard of his death two days ago. In the grand tradition of hard-living U.S. writers, he had taken his own life. But putting his own twist on it, he insisted that his earthly remains be fired out of a canon, a true gonzo send-off.

It would probably annoy Hunter to hear this—or anything I said—and it's extraordinarily sappy to say it, but I'm happy just to be able to say I met the man.

## DOUGLAS ADAMS
# A Galaxy Guide
# for Hitch Hikers Everywhere

"It seemed to me that any civilization that had so far lost its head as to need a set of detailed instructions for use in a package of toothpicks was no longer a civilization in which I could live and stay sane."

That could be the epitaph for author Doug Adams, who died of a massive heart attack on May 11, 2001, at the age of 49. I prefer to think that Adams, one of my favorite writers of all time, simply has joined one of his ever-resilient characters, Arthur Dent, hitchhiking through the cosmos, attempting to save Earth from destruction by Vogons to make room for an intergalactic freeway.

Adams' four-book "trilogy," which began with *The Hitch Hiker's Guide to the Galaxy* and ended with *So Long, and Thanks for All the Fish*, is a quirky collection of insights about life, disguised as a hilarious tale spread across the fabric of space and time.

The opening quotation actually comes from one of Adams' characters, Wonko the Sane, who withdrew from society after finding ridiculous instructions on a box of toothpicks. ("Hold stick near center of its length. Moisten pointed end in mouth. Insert in tooth space, blunt end next to gum. Use gentle in-and-out motion.")

Adams wrote that book nearly 20 years ago. He could not have known how much more crazy the world would get. Today, there would be a warning on the toothpick box advising you not to stick yourself in the eye.

Because of Adams, I became a reader of fine print. We have become so used to warnings on everything, from Q-tips ("Entering the ear canal could cause injury") to computer printer ink cartridges ("Do not drink"). We know, of course, that the detailed instructions and dire warnings are simply a ploy by manufacturers to avoid being sued. Corporation lawyers demand that such obvious dangers be stated in print because there are a few brain-dead people who *will* drink printer ink and jam a cotton swab into their brains through the ear canal.

Few of us even notice the warnings anymore. We know that only an idiot would strike a match without closing the cover. But we also know that there are a few people who have to be told to "Strike on back," even though the strike pad is only on the back of the matchbook. But do people really have to be warned that Zippo lighters "contain flammable gas under pressure"?

My shaving cream container warns users "not to spray toward open flame," a scenario that rarely comes up in a bathroom.

A warning on a box of staples states, "Handle with care. Staples have sharp points for penetration." Don't people know that? The main job of staples is to penetrate things, for which sharp points are mandatory.

Johnson's Baby Powder warns it is "for external use only," to keep, I suppose, people from using it as coffee creamer. And even Band-Aid bandages need a warning: "Package contains latex, which could cause allergic reaction."

I thought of Doug Adams while on my exercise bike, where there is a warning label that says in part, "Replace label if illegible or removed." Wonko the Sane might wonder how you can possibly replace something that is illegible or not even there at all.

The more I read the small print of life, the more I'm convinced that Doug Adams flagged down a passing starship, perhaps even one powered by an improbability drive, and headed for the restaurant at the end of the universe. So long, Doug, and thanks for all the books.

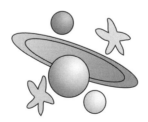

## PATRICK O'BRIAN
# Meeting a Man from an Earlier Time

KĀNEOHE, Hawai'i (Jan. 10, 2000)—Patrick O'Brian, who died at age 85 last week in Dublin, was probably the best writer you have never heard of.

You might say he wrote sailing novels, but that would be like saying Pablo Picasso drew pictures. O'Brian brought the Royal Navy of Admiral Nelson's day alive in a staggering series of books centered on two fictional characters, Capt. Jack Aubrey and his ship's surgeon Stephen Maturin. At the time of his death, O'Brian was working on the 21st installment of the Aubrey/Maturin series, which the *New York Times* called the best historical novels ever written.

Many who dipped a toe into the series found themselves swept overboard, eagerly awaiting each successive book and seasoning their daily speech with sea talk like, "Make a lane, mate, make a lane," "God rot your vitals, you infernal lubber" and the ever-popular drinking man's chorus, "The bottle stands by you, sir!" He is the reason I have a brass replica cannon and ship's lamp in my living room, not to mention a framed print of sailing ships over the fireplace and shelves of books devoted to Men of War, fighting frigates and great sea battles of the Napoleonic and Revolutionary wars. That's a lot of sea stuff for a guy who couldn't even handle four days on the *S.S. Constitution* between Hilo and Hanalei without getting seasick.

I joined the Cult of O'Brian in 1994 after the series was well underway. He wrote the first Aubrey/Maturin novel, *Master and Commander,* in 1960—to the collective yawn of the British public. But he became a hit in America. He counted actor Charlton Heston and television news legend Walter Cronkite among his fans. (His books later would become the basis of the movie *Master and Commander, The Far Side of the World,* starring Russell Crowe.)

The vivid detail of the Aubrey/Maturin series makes the more famous Horatio Hornblower novels by C.S. Forrester seem like crude sketches. O'Brian's depth of knowledge about life in the early 19th century was amazing, right down to what people ate. When lucky, his characters gorged on bizarrely-named puddings like Boiled Baby and Spotted Dog. When stores ran out, they lived on weevil-infested biscuits and millers, which basically were rats. "We call 'em millers to make 'em eat better," Capt. Aubrey explained to Dr. Maturin in *H.M.S. Surprise.*

O'Brian's books also found an American audience because at a time when no one seemed to be at the moral helm of the country O'Brian's characters acted with dignity, bravery and honor.

In *Wine Dark Sea*, after the crew survives a prodigious number of life-threatening incidents in the South Pacific, Maturin asks Aubrey if he ever considered just going home.

"'Yes, it often occurs to me, but then my innate nobility of character cries out, "Hey, Jack Aubrey: you mind your duty, do y'hear me there?" Do you know about duty, Stephen?'

'I believe I have heard it well spoken of.'

'Well, it exists.'"

In 1995, when O'Brian went to New York for a book signing, I convinced the *Honolulu Star-Bulletin*'s managing editor that it was absolutely imperative for me to interview O'Brian, although his books had nothing to do with Hawai'i. Basically, I wanted to be able to tell my grandkids that I actually talked with the gentleman.

I interviewed him by phone after being warned by his publisher not to actually ask any questions, because O'Brian believed question and answer is not a civilized form of conversation. Ha. O'Brian had tons of questions. He was interested in everything about Hawai'i, asking me things like, "The macadamia nut, what kind of tree does it grow on?" and "In Hawai'i, do they have many inland streams?" It was clear that he more closely identified with his character Dr. Maturin, the naturalist, physician and spy, than with the fighting ship captain, Aubrey. Our conversation was a bit strange. We both had bad colds and sniffled and sneezed through the whole thing. He suggested that a spot of rum probably would be good for both of us.

When not talking about Hawai'i's fish, streams and plants, he spoke of native Hawaiians. He was sensitive to the Hawaiian sovereignty movement, having spent a lot of time in Catalonia and Ireland, where sovereignty struggles have been going on for ages. "I perfectly understand the resistance of the Hawaiians," he said. "Very few people like to have their homelands invaded. There's an awful lot to be said for people just staying at home."

Being a very private man, O'Brian gave very few interviews. (Years later, I learned I was one of the few journalists he had talked to. I was even more surprised after that conversation when one of his books arrived in the mail, autographed.)

Eventually, O'Brian will be considered one of the literary giants of our time. But for now, a devoted handful of infernal lubbers will break out the Port and drink to his memory. Thankfully, he left many behind.

## SEPTEMBER 11, 2001
# Putting Life in Perspective

KĀNEOHE, Hawai'i (Sept. 12, 2001)—Nothing like the wholesale slaughter of several thousand innocent people to put your life into perspective.

I was worried about a lot of things a week ago, but for the life of me, I can't seem to remember what those things were. Something about money and not having enough of it, I suspect. One of our credit cards is a little high. I was probably worried about that. But then I saw the millions of pieces of paper blown out of the World Trade Center offices, representing the financial lives of thousands of people. The Manhattan streets looked like the devil threw a ticker-tape parade. Except, instead of confetti, the sky was filled with the fluttering sheets of peoples' existence: stock orders, inventory lists, personal checkbooks, savings accounts and, who knows, maybe even a laundry list. And as important as those little pieces of paper had been just days before, they were the farthest things from the minds of the victims' families and friends, and the rescuers.

So I must be wrong. I couldn't have been worried about one little credit card statement. One piece of paper. That would be absurd.

Maybe I was worried about the heat. It has been awfully hot in Hawai'i the last few weeks. But watching those firemen clad in stifling heavy protective coats, climbing up and down tons of cement and steel rubble, frying in the New York heat, I knew I must be wrong. I couldn't have possibly been worried about our heat.

Maybe I was worried that we had not had a good heavy rain in a long time. We need rain badly. But then I thought about the people trapped below the rubble in New York and the worries there that it would start raining. The rain would interfere with the rescue operation, possibly making a dangerous situation even worse. Suddenly, lack of rain seemed like a good thing.

I might have been worried about my health. I used to be a pretty good hypochondriac. As I've gotten older, I'm not really able to focus as well, at least not the kind of focus it takes to convince yourself that you've got a tumor growing somewhere on your body or are going through the early stages of mad cow disease. That's a young hypochondriac's game. But how could I have been worrying about my health at all when, unlike the thousands of victims of the World Trade Center destruction, I was still alive? Being alive is good. Being alive is something to be thankful for. You shouldn't waste being alive worrying that you might be putting on a few pounds or feeling guilty about having an extra slice of pizza.

I might have been worried about some argument I had with my wife. But is that possible? When two people live together for more than 20 years, someone's going to get on someone else's nerves, especially if that first someone is me. But a long, loving relationship is something to celebrate, and only an idiot would worry about a few bumps along the way.

A week ago, life was one big worry. Funny, today it's a blessing.

seven

# The Calabash Bowl

*"Life is much too important to take seriously."*
—Oscar Wilde

For instance, as you'll learn in this chapter, just a hundred years ago life expectancy was only 47 years. When you figure the first 10 years of that were wasted on childhood, it didn't leave a lot of time for partying. An important part of writing a humor column is the duty to get people to quit taking themselves, and life, so seriously. We are living in absolutely the best times in the history of the human race, measured by any standard you can name, except the use of cellular phones by SUV drivers. Here, then, is a calabash of offerings to hopefully remind you it's a wonderful life—and, for God's sake, lighten up.

# Poi Dogs

W e've always known that a lot of dogs look like their owners, which is one of the dirty tricks nature plays on unsuspecting canines.

Now there is a study to support something I've always suspected: that only purebred dogs look like their owners. Poi dogs—what mongrels are called here in Hawai'i—have too much self-respect to play those kinds of games.

Researchers at the University of California, with a laudable disregard for the things that many busybodies think need to be researched—global warming, the rain forest, the ozone hole, the ozone quadrangle, the ozone trapezoid, etc.—set about trying to figure out if it's true that dogs look like their owners and, if so, why; and, most importantly, would California taxpayers realize they were squandering public money on such an enterprise.

To the absolute surprise of no one who has ever bought or adopted a pooch, the reason that some dogs look like their owners is because it is the owners who pick out the dogs. Very rarely does a dog wander into a Human Humane Society and walk down rows of cages filled with pathetic-looking people until finally saying, "I'll take the geeky-looking dude with the red hair. Make sure he has all of his shots."

The researchers found that when people pick a dog, they look for one that, at some level, bears some resemblance to themselves, a wire report reportedly reported. But that applies mainly to people picking out purebred dogs. People who adopt poi dogs—or, to use the scientific name, mutts—apparently do not have the same "me, myself, my dog" psychosis as those who buy purebred dogs.

University psychology students examined dogs and their owners at various dog parks and found that while purebreds and their owners looked like the product of some bizarre breeding experiment, it seemed like the mutts and their owners arrived on separate buses. The students could not match up the mutts with their owners because many of the mutts wore sunglasses so as not to be recognized by their friends while being forced to hang out with human beings.

I actually proved this in 1997 when I staged the First Annual Real Poi Dog Contest at the Hawaiian Humane Society, a contest that has not been held annually ever since. We staged a number of competitions—sit, shake, roll over, naked Barbie fetch, quote the preamble to the U.S. Constitution, etc.—to find a real poi dog.

The competition was tough. If a dog ran and fetched the naked Barbie, he'd lose points. If he started to chase the Barbie but thought better of it, he'd lose fewer points. If he looked at the thrown Barbie with disdain and then lay down and began to groom himself in scandalous places, he won big points. If you said "shake" and the dog shook, he lost. If he sat on command, he lost. If he looked vaguely interested in what we were saying, points were deducted.

In the end, the winning Real Poi Dog was a nondescript mongrel who slept through the entire affair, rising only to surreptitiously relieve himself on the naked Barbie when the judges were tallying the points.

We never got that dog's name. Or found out who had brought him. He resembled no human other than Jack Nicholson, and that was only because of the sunglasses.

# When Stations Gave Service

I was filling up my truck with gas the other day, and the smell of the gasoline transported me back in time to when I worked at Steven's Super Service in 'Aiea, that small Leeward hillside town overlooking Pearl Harbor.

When I recall those high school days when service stations provided "service," I think it's probably better that people pump their own gas today.

I was a hardworking little punk, but I really didn't grasp the particulars of working around automobiles, especially at a place like Steven's, right on busy Kamehameha Highway, where so many cars came in it was like working in a NASCAR pit. While filling up a car's radiator with water one day, I noticed that his engine looked awfully hot. So I sprayed the water hose on it to cool it off. Steam and smoke began pouring out of the engine. I shut the hood quickly. I learned later that the technical term for what I had probably done was "cracking the engine block." I sent the driver back into the race on Kam Highway hoping he wouldn't notice the steam coming out from under the hood.

I never actually told my boss, Mr. Yoshioka, about that incident. He was on hand, however, when I set a customer's car engine on fire. It was an accident, of course. The boss didn't want to hear about the nasty shock I received when I inadvertently touched the metal oil dipstick to a hot wire by the engine. A fire at a gas station tends to make everyone edgy.

What I lacked in technical expertise, I tried to make up in hustle.

I was washing the windows of one car so fast that I didn't notice the driver's window was down. Personally, I thought the driver overreacted. I mean, it was just a sponge. The boss urged me not to punch the customers in the face while cleaning their windows.

The boss had a large map of O'ahu on the office door. He loved that map. While racing into the office to get some change one day I slipped. As I went down, my fingers caught the top of the boss' map and ripped a four-inch swath down the length of it. The boss was extremely disappointed.

We were lowly gas monkeys. But we were called on to do things that seemed beyond the scope of our responsibilities.

Next to the gas station, we stored cars that had been involved in accidents or recovered by police on the Leeward side of the island. Tow trucks brought them in night and day. Sometimes we were asked to remove any valuables and lock the cars. Once, when I was reaching across a pool of blood to retrieve a jacket, something soft fell on my arm from the broken windshield. I'm not sure what it was, but it had hair. I think asking some kid making $1.35 an hour to deal with death cars and pools of blood was a bit too much. This was a gas station, damn it, not CSI.

If someone couldn't pay for their gas, we were supposed to make the person leave his spare tire. This struck me as being a dangerous responsibility when the boss wasn't around. Especially the night a stolen car full of young toughs came in. I noticed there was no key in the ignition, but filled the car up anyway. As I recall, the following conversation then took place:

**Me:** That'll be eight dollars.

**Driver:** Sorry, brah, I no more money. (Smiling at his buddies.) I wen' forget my wallet.

**Me**: Well, I'm supposed to take the spare tire.

**Driver:** (indicating the hot wires): Yeah, but, I no more trunk key, eh?

**Me:** Well, you guys have a nice night, okay?

Had I been wearing a Kevlar vest, I might have been a bit more aggressive in trying to get the spare tire. But Kevlar wasn't invented yet, and I was pretty sure that Chevron patch on my shirt wouldn't stop a bullet.

When the boss and I opened the station early each morning, it was still dark. Throughout the morning, the boss would chew on his unlit cigar as we put out the oilcans, waited on cars and cleaned the restrooms.

Finally, the sun would come up and the boss and I would sit on the little white wall in front of the office. We'd look out over Pearl Harbor. The water would be like glass and the sky golden. Sailboats rocked gently in a marina, and Ford Island seemed to float in the middle of the harbor. At those times, everything seemed right with the world. The boss would finally light the uneaten part of his cigar, take a deep puff and say "Charley boy, go school. Study hard. Don't be like me: work every day, fall asleep during football games on TV." It was good advice. But he also could have told me not to touch hot wires with a metal dipstick.

# Our Little Shop of (Tax) Horrors

As America's "Boutique State," Hawai'i is the most expensive place in the country to live. And it should be that way.

When you go to one of those cute little specialty shops tucked away on an expensive backstreet of Waikīkī, you can't expect to pay Costco prices for precious little knick-knacks and doo-dads.

On the mainland, New York is the bustling center of commerce; Florida is one big gated community and retirement home; the South a rugged, hot, rural zone of chiggers, cheap booze and firecracker stands; California is one big strip mall; the Northwest is a forest preserve; and Hawai'i...well, Hawai'i is that expensive little boutique state that you visit when you have some spare cash to blow.

Except for those of us who live here. We have to pay premium prices for frivolous knick-knacks and doo-dads such as food, clothing and shelter. And we pay taxes. Taxes are what keeps Hawai'i lookin' good, attracting the New York business types, the chigger-scratching southerners and the California car dealers to our little specialty state.

The U.S. Census Bureau just released a report confirming what anyone who lives here knows: that Hawai'i residents pay more per person in state taxes than any other state. The Hawai'i state income tax form could be edited down to just two lines: 1. How much money did you make in the preceding taxable year? 2. Send it to us.

But then we wouldn't have any money to pay real estate taxes, gas taxes, excise taxes and the various assessments, duties, tariffs and levies that are the cost of living on a tiny speck of land in the Pacific.

I'm not complaining. Anyone who moves to Hawai'i voluntarily should be soaked for every penny they possess. I could be running a firecracker shack on the Texas/Oklahoma border, living in a double-wide trailer and figuring how many seconds it takes to sprint from the kitchen to the tornado bunker in the back yard. I choose to be skinned financially in order to live in the most beautiful place on Earth.

I do, however, feel some sympathy for the original inhabitants of the Islands who didn't ask for their home to be turned into a mecca for the moneyed classes.

State taxes should be pro-rated, based on how many generations your family has been in Hawai'i. That won't happen because Hawai'i needs to squeeze as much money as possible out of every living inhabitant, and, come to think about it, the dead ones, too.

Although we pay more in state taxes than anyone else, it could be worse and probably will be. One day we'll pay a county tax, town tax, neighborhood tax, street-you-live-on tax and "bed-you-sleep-in" tax.

Face it. When it comes to states, Hawai'i is like a high-maintenance girlfriend (or cross-dressing boyfriend). States like West Virginia, New Jersey and Mississippi can plod around without makeup in pajamas and hair curlers. Hawai'i has to look gorgeous in the morning.

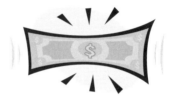

# Living with Creepy-Crawlies

There apparently are some unwanted visitors to Schofield Barracks, the central Oʻahu army base tucked along the scenic Waiʻanae mountain range. Some of the military families assigned there from the Mainland are disturbed by some of our little furry island friends who visit the post, namely rats.

One woman complained that a rat ate her pet parrot. That's surprising. I've never heard of a rat eating a parrot. I thought they were partial to canaries.

Another woman complained that not only are there rats, there are also termites, ants and cockroaches. Which raises the question: What, no centipedes?

It's hard to move from the mainland to a tropical place where it seems that everything outdoors wants to come indoors. Schofield officials have tried to explain to military families that having critters running around is part of life on a tropical island. But it's one thing to be told about Asian cockroaches, and another to see one of the monsters pushing over your trashcan.

I think our military guests to the Islands need a short primer for handling the local wildlife. I hope this helps:

1. Everything in Hawaiʻi is either eating or being eaten. That includes your house. A house is simply a very expensive piece of termite food. Termites live underground until breeding time, when they swarm out into the night sky and make hoochie-koochie in numbers that would make Alfred Hitchcock freak out. Don't panic; they don't bite. People. They are attracted to light, so if you turn off all the lights in your house, they'll fly to your neighbors' house.

2. We don't have snakes in Hawaiʻi. We do have mongooses. A mongoose is like a 2-foot-long rat with a long nose and sharp teeth. They were brought to Hawaiʻi to kill rats, but the two species apparently made a deal to leave each other alone. Now we have both mongooses and rats, so their deal worked

out pretty well.

3. There are two types of rats in Hawai'i: the kind that live in your house and the kind that live in your garage. They eat anything (See: Parrot, above). We once found a rat hanging by his teeth in the back of our clothes dryer. He apparently electrocuted himself while lunching on a hot wire. The only way to deal with a rat is to trap it. The snap traps are effective, but kind of gruesome. (Nothing like waking up to a smashed rat head in your kitchen.) The live cage traps work, but then you have to deal with the rascals later. I usually blindfold them and take them on a long ride in my truck. Then spin them around three times fast and leave them in a remote area. They hardly ever find their way back home after that.

4. The big black birdlike things that come into your house at night are cockroaches. They, too, are attracted to light, but also food. It's best just to shoot these things with guns. You folks on Schofield probably have the necessary firepower. I suggest something in the .45 caliber range. Twenty-twos will just annoy them. And be careful, they charge when they're wounded.

5. Ants. They're everywhere. What can you do? Clean your dishes as soon as you're done eating. Better yet, eat on your driveway. Don't leave out a scrap of food anywhere (this will deter the roaches, too.) Buy a truck load of ziplock-type plastic bags and keep everything in them, from bread to crackers. Heck, get the super-large size and zip up your refrigerator. Don't bother to spray ants with insecticide; it only excites them and causes them to call for reinforcements.

6. Most of all, enjoy your tour of duty in lovely Hawai'i. And keep moving.

# A Bridge Too Far

I've been reading the "Bridge" column on the *Honolulu Star-Bulletin* comics page for nearly 20 years, and I still don't know what the hell that card game all about. It's like reading the ravings of a lunatic or some secret World War II memo written in code to hide the actual details of a planned invasion.

To those non-bridge players like me, the column is devoted to various strategies employed in what supposedly is the most popular card game of all time. I say "supposedly," because I've only met two bridge players in my entire life; one was a 19-year-old intellectual wacko and the other was the oldest ambulatory person I'd ever seen.

I suppose the game is popular, because it's the only card game given a major chunk of newspaper real estate every day. I read the column in awe. Rarely are so many words from the English language strung together in sentences that fail to elicit any cognitive brain function.

Here's a sample sentence from a typical bridge column:

"East wins the diamond ace while the North invades the South near Vicksburg and the Dummy's club foot trips on the five of spades, over-tricking the defenders while West's heart king sneaks off for a few tricks of his own with club queen who turns out to be a jack in queen's clothing (so the king was surprised there) and the defender trumps the Dummy's bid and switches to the Green Party while East makes his contract but goes Chapter 11 anyhow and the South shall rise again."

If you think that doesn't make sense, you should see the chart that goes along with it. Bridge columns always have a chart showing all the cards in everyone's hand, including the Dummy, which seems to be a cruel thing to call a fellow card player. But that's the way bridge is. It seems like a quiet, dignified and sophisticated game played by the only people in the world who eat tiny cucumber sandwiches without the crust. But it's actually a vicious game whereby contestants are constantly attacking, defending, clubbing, spading, killing and, apparently, ruffing the tricker.

I will likely be hearing from hardcore bridge players after writing this. They will call me a booby, chump, clod, dimwit, dolt, dullard and big dummy because that's the way bridge players see people who don't know how to play their game.

There has been talk over the years of stopping the bridge column because no poll of subscribers has actually turned up an actual bridge-column reader. But no editor has had the guts to do it. I think they sense that there is something more to the bridge column than meets the eye. That it is part of some cosmic glue that holds the cosmos together.

(Personally, I suspect something more sinister: that bridge players secretly control the world and the bridge column actually is the way they communicate with each other and dispatch their secret forces around the globe.)

The bridge column was, is and forever shall be, so help us God. But that doesn't mean we can't have other columns devoted to card games. Frankly, a good column on blackjack would serve Hawai'i readers well. So many Hawai'i residents go to Las Vegas, they probably could use advice like, "When the dealer is showing a 4 and you've got a 9 or 10, double down." Or, "Always split aces." Or, "Keep your eyes on your cards, not the dealer's breasts." Or, "Don't have another rum and Coke, you idiot, you're already down $500."

See, that's the kind of information the average Hawai'i card player needs to know.

# Gadgets Behaving Badly

I t's long been known that predatory animals can smell fear. Now it appears that certain machines and electronic devices can smell distrust by users and react negatively. Anyone facing a deadline on a long report or project only to have the computer printer crash as if on cue knows of this phenomenon.

My wife and I recently made the mistake of discussing out loud our plans to sell her car while riding in said vehicle, only to have the thing suddenly develop a serious mechanical malady cured only by $300 in repairs. The car clearly resented our lack of support and contrived to punish us before we could put it on the market. If only we had communicated in discreet nudges and winks, the car would have been none the wiser and we $300 richer.

Computers are highly susceptible to bad vibes being given off by the user. How many times has your computer shut down in a snit simply because you thought it wasn't working fast enough? I was writing a column on this very computer about the moodiness of computers not long ago when (and I mean this in the least offensive way possible, Mr. Computer) it went from iMac to iQuit in midsentence. Since then, I daily express my undying love and admiration for it, and it's working like a champ. Good iMac, good boy!

Large appliances, in particular, react badly to criticism or perceived perfidy. My friend was considering getting a new washing machine only to come home from work to find that his disheartened Maytag had popped off its hose and filled his house with water for several hours.

Researchers at Princeton University have in fact released a study that purports to show that machines behave badly when they sense bad vibes by users.

"There are some people who seem to have a natural rapport with computers and other complex machines, and there are other people who seem to break everything without touching it," one of the researchers said.

To put all the blame on the user's attitude seems unfair. I've found that, historically, it's the machine's behavior that first sends me reaching for a baseball bat.

The researchers say users of mechanical and electronic devices "seem to change the output of the machines simply by thinking about them."

That would clearly imply the machines are thinking about the users right back and reacting in a petulant manner. (Not you, Mr. iMac, I'm talking about that insolent ceiling fan over there.)

# A Bad Call

It turns out that cellular phone use is the No. 1 cause of newspaper editorials about automobile accidents. A recent national survey showed that eight out of 10 newspaper editorials regarding traffic accidents mentioned cell phones. It's clear that if people would stop using cell phones in their cars, newspapers would stop writing editorials about traffic accidents, or something like that.

My paper, the *Honolulu Star-Bulletin*, had a great editorial about the connection between cell phones and auto accidents. It was full of all the numbers editorial writers are required to use under the Federal Editorial Writers Mandatory Data Utilization Act of 1914. Columnists are under no such restraints and, indeed, see statistics, research data and other hairy facts as impediments to lively writing. (For instance, I referred to the *Star-Bulletin* as "my paper" when I don't even own it.)

Anyway, I rapidly scanned in-depth recent articles and editorials concerning cell phones and automobiles and determined that the general beef is:

1. You don't use a car in your office, so you shouldn't use your cell phone in your car.
2. Cellular phones are a distraction while driving, particularly if you have them set on vibrate and the phone is deep in your pocket and you're listening to a Barry White CD when you receive a phone call.
3. Driving a car is not like participating in a circus act. Increasing the difficulty of driving by talking on cellular phones, wearing a blindfold or balancing a Chinese acrobat on your head is not necessary.

These are all good points. Where I diverge from my periodical pundit pals is the contention that using a cell phone while driving is somehow worse than doing other things while driving. Using a cellular phone while driving might even save your life. Say you're talking to one of those Caribbean Psychic Network ladies and she's flipping over Tarot cards and says, "I see danger, my brother. Your girlfriend is cheating on you and you're about to slam head-on into truck full of large, angry tree trimmers from some exotic Polynesian isle." You swerve out of the way of the oncoming truck with less than a second to spare.

I'm not sticking up for people who use their phones while driving. I think they are idiots. Well, I think most drivers are idiots, including me. I've used a cell phone while driving but I swear I do not listen to Barry White. (And I only drove with an acrobat on my head once.)

But there are so many other dangerous things people do while driving. I drove on a couple of occasions with a steaming cup of Starbucks regular drip between my legs. They put those little plastic lids on the cups but there's a hole in the lid that directs searing hot liquid in a stream directly to the part of your body where it can do the most damage whenever you hit a bump. There's a TV commercial that says your day doesn't start until you get a little "Folgers in your cup." Trust me. You haven't kicked off the morning until you've had a little "Starbucks in your lap."

So, yes, people shouldn't use cell phones while driving. They shouldn't do anything while driving but drive. We don't need to outlaw phone use in cars, we need to outlaw idiots in cars. And that's going to be very tough.

# The Hawai'i Quarter

The *Honolulu Star-Bulletin* challenged readers to come up with designs for the "Hawai'i" quarter the U.S. Mint will be issuing in 2008. And, can you believe it, not one person suggested that the coin feature a mongoose, gecko or cockroach.

Most of the suggestions ran to the old clichéd island stuff like Diamond Head, surfing, King Kamehameha and a pineapple. Those buying into this vein of thought probably would think the perfect design for a Hawai'i quarter would be King Kamehameha surfing with a pineapple under his arm and Diamond Head in the background. Please. Let's not promote the Hollywood version of the Islands on our quarter. Let's tell the real story.

First of all, it shouldn't be a quarter at all. It should be a 50-cent piece, because everything costs twice as much in Hawai'i as it does on the mainland.

Secondly, it should have attitude. A mongoose gnashing his teeth with an angry glint in his eye would set Hawai'i's coin apart from the other states'. Name another state where residents would consider a foot-long rodent "cute."

Likewise, what other state would allow reptiles the size of your hand to wander at will through the house? But geckos not only are allowed in the house, they are encouraged to enter to eat the bugs that already have set up camp in there. A good quarter design would be a gecko, his stomach engorged with termites, winking at the world.

Some would say that a cockroach doesn't belong on a quarter. Well, a cockroach doesn't belong in the silverware drawer, either, but he manages to get in there often enough. A cockroach quarter would be cool, especially if the bug is in surf trunks on a wave with Diamond Head in the background. (Pineapple optional.)

A killer quarter design would feature all three creatures—mongoose, gecko and cockroach. I imagine something like the mongoose and gecko fighting with canoe paddles and the cockroach acting as the referee.

Because Hawai'i is surrounded by water, we might also want to consider an ocean-related design for the quarter. How about a swimmer running across the surface of the water with a tiger shark in hot pursuit and Diamond Head in the background? (Pineapple optional.) Or a shark wearing a gaudy aloha shirt and sunglasses hanging out on a Waikīkī street corner surreptitiously checking out the biped buffet? Or a shark flashing a shaka sign with the motto (in Hawaiian) "A Haole a Day Keeps the Doctor Away"? Anyway, something along the shark line should be included on the Hawai'i quarter.

I got it. A mongoose, gecko, cockroach and shark sitting at a table playing cards, like that famous card-playing dog painting. But each of our critters will be eyeballing their neighbor like they're all planning to eat one another. Now that's the real Hawai'i: Everything is a meal for something else.

# Honolulu's Hundred Years

A mainland reader, perhaps noting our Sunday coverage of Honolulu's centennial tomorrow, sent me a list of statistics from the year 1905 to remind us all how much (or how little) things have changed in 100 years.

In the year 1905...

- The average life expectancy was 47 years. *(When you were 47, you looked 80; when you were 30, you looked 60; and when you were 13, you looked like Sir Bob Geldof today.)*
- The maximum speed limit in most cities was 10 mph. *(Which happens to be the maximum speed reached today on the H-1 freeway during "rush" hour.)*
- Only 8% of homes had a telephone. *(Today, 100% of homes in Hawai'i have eight phones.)*
- Only 14% of homes had a bathtub. *(Bathers were very friendly back then.)*
- The tallest structure in the world was the Eiffel Tower. *(The second tallest was William Howard Taft. The Aloha Tower, built in 1926, was the tallest structure in Hawai'i but was hardly used because no one needed a 10-story one-bedroom apartment. )*
- The average wage was 22 cents per hour. *(Of course, the average hour was only 22 minutes.)*
- More than 95% of all births took place at home. *(Back then, HMO stood for "Help Mom Operate.")*
- About 90% of doctors had no college education. *(Which might explain the home birthrate.)*
- Coffee was 15 cents a pound. *(The most popular coffee shop was called Starcents.)*
- Most women washed their hair only once a month and used borax or egg yolks for shampoo. *(In Hawai'i, women washed their hair with poi, pineapple juice and coconut milk, thus the birth of the derogatory term "lū'au head.")*
- Diarrhea was the third leading cause of death. *(The fourth was

*living next door to someone so afflicted.)*
- The American flag had only 45 stars. *(Hawai'i was granted a star in 1959, even though we specifically requested a smiley face.)*
- Hawai'i, Arizona, Oklahoma, New Mexico and Alaska hadn't been admitted to the Union yet. *(They were waiting for Alabama, Mississippi and Tennessee to secede.)*
- The population of Las Vegas was only 30. *(That year, the World Series of Poker was still known as the World Series of Solitaire.)*
- Two out of 10 adults couldn't read or write. *(On the bright side, they were doctors.)*
- Marijuana, heroin and morphine were available over the counter at corner drugstores. *(Now they are all available at corner drug dealers.)*
- There were only 230 murders reported in the entire United States. *(Today there are 230 reported murders a year in police stations alone.)*

All joking aside, it's amazing to see how far we've come in only 100 years. Imagine: Today a 55-year-old man (with a life expectancy of 110) could call the hospital from one of his eight phones, then whisk his 60-year-old pregnant wife out of one of their five bathtubs and drive 100 mph to a hospital where a doctor who actually graduated from college will deliver a child who will soon be paid $10 minimum wage to deliver $6 coffees to diarrhea-free corner marijuana dealers. What a world!

## eight

# Charleyisms

*"Instead of swords, why didn't the Three Musketeers use muskets?"*
—Charles Memminger

Some people say there's more than one way to skin a cat. But they never offer details.

Feng shui is the ancient Chinese science of getting people to pay a lot of money to have their furniture rearranged.

A news story said, "A shark was spotted off the Waikīkī groin." I don't know about you, but I never like to see the words "shark" and "groin" in the same sentence.

I suffer from Pre-Traumatic Stress Syndrome. It's like Post-Traumatic Stress Syndrome, except instead of stressing out from something bad that has happened to you, you stress out over all the millions of bad things that *could* happen to you.

When I was a kid in school, they started off the day by broadcasting the Pledge of Allegiance over the public address system. Today it's the Miranda Warning.

Prostitution is the only profession where practitioners have to learn not only the tricks of the trade but the trade of the tricks.

I'm all for protecting endangered species. Especially if they taste good.

I've got two major problems: I never forget a face and I can never remember a name.

If you are going to be in the business of executing cows and converting them into sandwiches sold by a guy in a clown costume, you should be well beyond caring what an animal rights organization has to say about it.

The number-one rule of ranching: never raise anything that's hard to catch.

I'm the only writer in the country who can generate hate mail for saying Steve Forbes is goofy-looking.

You have to be rich to be eccentric; otherwise you're just some crazy person who dresses funny.

Bacon is the tobacco of food. When you eat bacon in public, people stare at you as if you are opening up your chest with a rusty machete.

The number of empty parking spaces at a mall decreases in direct proportion to how badly a driver looking for an empty parking space has to pee.

If you can keep your head while those around you are losing theirs, you probably don't understand the magnitude of the problem.

It's well known that days in Hawai'i get shorter in winter. That's because it rains so much, the days get wet and shrink.

When my daughter was three, I asked her to name the major holidays. She said, "Halloween, Christmas, Thankgoodness and Disneyland."

I think cockfighting not only should be legal, but mandatory. For all chickens. Wouldn't you feel better knowing the bird responsible for your teriyaki chicken sandwich died in the glory of battle instead of being executed like a common criminal?

Running is bad for you. I don't know anyone who runs a lot who is not afflicted by a bad back, wrecked knees and an insufferable ego.

Something should be added to the game of chess to make it interesting to watch. Like mace.

I can't believe they banned Lawn Darts. They were just these foot-long, metal-tipped winged missiles that you flung across the yard in the general direction of your friend.

Anti-religious types don't think Good Friday should be a holiday. I say, look at it this way: Pretend it's just short for "GOOD—I don't have to work on—FRIDAY."

Ah, the Kentucky Derby. The only time of the year when otherwise normal people say "gelding" and "furlong" and use the word "chestnut" as a color.

Somehow the lipstick industry manages to stay just ahead of dishwasher detergent makers in a race for the strongest product.

Scientists can trace all mankind to one woman in Africa 200,000 years ago. They can trace all dogs back to a single dog in Africa about the same time. The question is, was he that woman's dog?

I hate haikus. They are like crummy little collections of words that couldn't make the limericks team.

Spunkiness has been bred out of cows. All they do now is stand around and look disinterested in life, which is not a bad attitude to have for a future hamburger steak.

It's a fundamental law of car radio dynamics that as soon as you turn on your radio, you'll hear the last four bars of your favorite song.

The best New Year's resolutions are the ones you make in June. By then you've had enough time to see how the year is playing out.

Eventually, everyone will be a guest on a television cooking show. It's simple mathematics.

When I was a kid, I dreamed of being something fearless, like a fireman or a commodities trader.

I'm not the best speller in the world. I always considered spelling a weird hang-up propagated by that anal-retentive guy Webster just to sell a few books.

What can you say about a language where this sentence makes sense? "The new gnu knew which witch a night knight might now know, but not which waves waifs waive when surfing serfs, where we were, wear wire ware at noon and from one to two, too."

Write this down: Never put anything in writing. You'll just regret it later.